S0-AXI-922

Forever Rich

Other books by David Servant

Forgive Me for Waiting so Long to Tell You This

Through the Needle's Eye

HeavenWord Daily

The Great Gospel Deception

The Disciple-Making Minister

FOREVER
RICH

Seven Scriptural Secrets to
Ultimate Financial Fulfillment

David Servant

ETHNOS PRESS
Pittsburgh, Pennsylvania

Forever Rich
Seven Scriptural Secrets to Ultimate Financial Fulfillment
First Printing: June 2012

Copyright © 2012 by David Servant. All rights reserved. No portion of this book may be reproduced in any form without the written permission of the copyright owner, except for brief excerpts quoted in critical reviews.

All Scripture quotations in this book, except those noted otherwise, are from the New American Standard Bible, © 1960, 1962, 1963, 1971,1972, 1973, 1975, and 1977 by The Lockman Foundation, and are used by permission.

Cover Design: CJ McDaniel
Printed in the United States of America
International Standard Book Numbers: 978-0-9827656-1-6 and 978-0-9827656-2-3

Table of Contents

Introduction

You are going to love this story. Jesus told it using just one sentence, but with a little imagination, it can easily be expanded without doing any harm to the lesson.

A man is walking across a neighbor's field early one morning when something poking through the soil—perhaps exposed from last night's rain shower—catches his attention. He stops. With the aid of his staff, he digs around it to uncover an old, metal chest. Wrenching the lid open, he discovers thousands of gold coins. It's a treasure buried long ago, perhaps by a prince or king who was fleeing from a foreign army.

He thinks to himself, "If I owned this field, I would own this treasure." So he quickly covers the chest and makes his way to the home of the field's owner.

"Good morning, my old friend Tobiah! I was just walking through your field and I was thinking to myself what a nice field it is. Have you ever considered selling it?"

"No, my friend, Yitzhak, it's not for sale, and I have never thought of selling it. It was an inheritance from my father, and that field helps me feed my eleven children."

"Well, yes, of course brother Tobiah. But what if someone was to pay you a very good price for your field…say twice the going rate per acre? Could that motivate you to sell it?"

Tobiah perceives that he has a highly-motivated buyer on the hook. "Well, my dear friend, Yitzhak, I'm afraid twice the going rate would not be *quite* enough. For me to be motivated to sell that field, well, it would take quite an offer. That field has been in our family for generations."

"Then how about three times the going rate per acre?"

Tobiah almost swallows his Adam's apple as he tries to keep his exuberance hidden. "Hmmm, that is a pretty persuasive offer." He momentarily wonders why Yitzhak is so motivated to buy his field, but the thought of selling it for three times its value overpowers his concern. He knows that if he sells his field at that price, he can immediately buy another field three times its size. Tobiah looks at Yitzhak's hopeful face and inwardly debates if he should risk demanding even more.

"I'll tell you what I'll do. I don't really want to sell it, but, because you're a friend and neighbor, I think I could let it go to you for *four* times the going rate. But that is my lowest price. My wife was just saying the other day how much she loves that field. I'm going to have to answer to her if I sell it."

Yitzhak grabs Tobiah's hand and shakes it vigorously. "Then we've got a deal!" Tobiah watches incredulously as Yitzhak briskly walks away. "What a fool!" he thinks to himself. Meanwhile, Yitzhak inwardly shouts, "What a wise man am I!"

When Yitzhak arrives home, he tells his wife the good news. They immediately begin to liquidate everything they own in order to raise the cash needed to buy Tobiah's field. In a few weeks, everything is gone. Their home, field, barn, cows, horses, furniture, and tools have all been sold to neighbors—who have all been talking about Yitzhak's foolishness behind his back.

Finally the day of the sale arrives. Yitzhak buys Tobiah's field for his exorbitant price and holds the deed in his hand. The hidden treasure now belongs to him. He's suddenly wealthier than he ever dreamed of being. The "fool" is no fool at all. He paid just a fraction of the field's true worth.

Here's how Jesus told the story:

The kingdom of heaven is like a treasure hidden in the field, which a man found and hid; and from joy over it he goes and sells all that he has, and buys that field (Matt. 13:44).

Clearly, Jesus was not trying to teach us that the kingdom could be gained without cost. The very essence of following Christ is self-denial—but self-denial *with a view to a reward*, something that Jesus Himself exemplified (Heb. 12:2). He who endured the cross for the joy set before Him told His followers that they would save their lives by losing them for His and the gospel's sake (Mark 8:35). Eternal gains are ours through temporary loss. And the kingdom of heaven is like a treasure so valuable that it is worth giving up everything to gain it.

Of course, the general self-denial required of those who will inherit God's kingdom (as illustrated in Jesus' Parable of the Hidden Treasure) is expressed through consistent daily acts of self-denial, and it is those consistent acts that will be proportionately rewarded. This is certainly true concerning any *monetary* sacrifice that we make, as Jesus said at another time:

Do not store up for yourselves treasures on earth, where moth and rust destroy, and where thieves break in and steal. But store up for yourselves treasures in heaven, where neither moth nor rust destroys, and where thieves do not break in or steal; for where your treasure is, there your heart will be also (Matt. 6:19-21).

We have the alternative of laying up our treasures on earth—where we will inevitably forfeit them before or at our death—or in heaven, where they will never be lost. We are faced with the same decision as the man who discovered the hidden treasure in his neighbor's field, and it is similarly a "no-brainer."

The Wisest Investment

Although mothballs, rust-resistant paints and home security systems might help modern followers of Christ counteract the work of moths, rust and thieves, the timeless wisdom of Jesus' words stands. Modern wealth evaporates all the time through currency inflation, bad investments and obsolete electronic gadgets. Storing up treasure in heaven is the wisest investment anyone can make for several reasons, one of which is that it eliminates all risk of loss. As martyred missionary Jim Elliot so wisely wrote, "He is no fool who gives up what he cannot keep to gain what he cannot lose." And that is what this little book is all about—becoming *forever rich.*

Forever goes beyond death, which is something far too few of us think about. Financial planners often consider the grave to be life's terminal point, but that is the ultimate *grave error.* According to Jesus, we can and should plan for our financial future beyond this life. In light of the fact that our earthly sojourn is but a blink in eternity, we are wise to be more focused on the next life, on *forever.*

Imagine that you were given a million dollars, concerning which your benefactor only made one requirement: With that money, you must purchase two houses, one in which you must live for a day, and the other in which you must live for the rest of your life.

If you spent $990,000 on the one-day house, very few people who knew of your decision would be seeking your investment advice. In fact, if you spent $500,000 on each home, most observers would be shaking their heads. A wise person would spend as little as possible on his one-day house. He might consider living in a doghouse for a day! That way, he could enjoy the nicest possible house for the remaining years of his life.

True Riches

The path to being *forever rich* begins in this life, and the benefits begin here as well. You don't have to wait until heaven to start enjoying all of the blessings. But we must begin to look at wealth from Jesus' perspective, a perspective that runs counter to the world's wisdom. He often sees poverty in what most consider wealth, and wealth in what most consider poverty. He once told a church full of materially rich people that they were poor (see Rev. 3:17). That is, they were spiritually and eternally poor. Yet Jesus told another church of impoverished people that they were rich (see Rev. 2:9).

Jesus' perspective is often radically different than ours, isn't it? He looks at things from an *eternal* perspective.

All of this is to say that, when we measure wealth only by earthly money and possessions, we're making a significant error, and we reveal an understanding that is a *mis*understanding. Becoming *forever rich* requires a change of perspective, a renewing of our minds, and a re-appraisal of what we currently value.

This is a book that will guide you along the path to becoming truly rich, now and forever, all based on what Jesus taught. Think of it as a treasure map. Let's get started.

CHAPTER ONE

Jesus, Venture Capitalist

There is no one like Jesus! Scripture reveals Him as the King of kings, Lord of lords, Son of God, Savior, Messiah, Prince of Peace and Light of the World—titles of which He alone is worthy. But did you know that He is also revealed in the Bible as being a venture capitalist?

A venture capitalist is a wealthy person who invests in new businesses. He takes the risk of losing his investment if a new business in which he invests fails, but if it succeeds, he profits significantly. Jesus revealed Himself as being such an investor in His Parable of the Talents:

> For it is just like a man about to go on a journey, who called his own slaves and entrusted his possessions to them. To one he gave five talents, to another, two, and to another, one, each according to his own ability; and he went on his journey. Immediately the one who had received the five talents went and traded with them, and gained five more talents. In the same manner the one who had received the two talents gained two more. But he who received the one talent went away, and dug a hole in the ground and hid his master's money.
>
> Now after a long time the master of those slaves came and settled accounts with them. The one who had received the five talents came up and brought five more talents, saying, "Master, you entrusted five talents to me. See, I have

gained five more talents." His master said to him, "Well done, good and faithful slave. You were faithful with a few things, I will put you in charge of many things; enter into the joy of your master."

Also the one who had received the two talents came up and said, "Master, you entrusted two talents to me. See, I have gained two more talents." His master said to him, "Well done, good and faithful slave. You were faithful with a few things, I will put you in charge of many things; enter into the joy of your master."

And the one also who had received the one talent came up and said, "Master, I knew you to be a hard man, reaping where you did not sow and gathering where you scattered no seed. And I was afraid, and went away and hid your talent in the ground. See, you have what is yours."

But his master answered and said to him, "You wicked, lazy slave, you knew that I reap where I did not sow and gather where I scattered no seed. Then you ought to have put my money in the bank, and on my arrival I would have received my money back with interest. Therefore take away the talent from him, and give it to the one who has the ten talents. For to everyone who has, more shall be given, and he will have an abundance; but from the one who does not have, even what he does have shall be taken away. Throw out the worthless slave into the outer darkness; in that place there will be weeping and gnashing of teeth" (Matt. 25:14-30).

Obviously, the master in the parable represents Jesus, who has given us everything we own and before whom we must all one day appear to give an account (see 2 Cor. 5:10). The slaves represent followers of Christ, whom the Bible often refers as His bond-servants (for example, Rev. 1:1). And the talents, each equivalent to two year's wages for an average workman in Christ's day, clearly represent everything that Jesus has entrusted to us to use for His purposes. They are thus considered by most commentators to represent our opportunities, abilities and money, or, as it is often said, our time, talents and treasures.

Some commentators downplay our accountability in regard to one of those three, namely, our money. Surely, however, it would be unwise to conclude that the *money* in Jesus' parable symbolizes everything that He has entrusted to us *besides* money.

All of this is to say that Jesus is very much like a venture capitalist. He's entrusted to all of His servants different amounts of His money with which we are to do His business.

He expects a return on His investments, and one day we'll have to give an account. Those who have done well will be proportionately rewarded. Those who have been unfaithful will, like the third slave in Jesus' parable, forfeit everything.

> Am I ready to stand before Him to give an account of my stewardship?

That being so, we are wise to ask ourselves, *Am I doing what Jesus expects of me with the money He has entrusted to me? Am I bringing Him a return on His investment? Is His kingdom being furthered because of my stewardship? Am I ready to stand before Him to give an account of my stewardship?*

The answers to those questions reveal what our eternal future holds for us.

The Grave Consequences of Poor Stewardship

I must confess my profound concern that too many professing Christians are glossing over a very sobering message that this parable seeks to amplify. That concern constrains me not to hide what Jesus so clearly reveals, even if I risk losing some readers in this, our first chapter together. Please, I sincerely ask, open your heart and mind and read the remainder of this chapter thoughtfully and carefully. It lays a foundation upon which every other principle is built on the journey to becoming *forever rich*.

Take note that the third slave in Jesus' parable, whom his master referred to as being *wicked*, *lazy* and *worthless*, was punished for his unfaithfulness by being cast into the "outer darkness… where there is weeping and gnashing of teeth" (Matt. 25:30). That sounds very much like hell, doesn't it?

Because the third servant in Jesus' parable certainly appears to represent someone who, like the other two servants, had a relationship with God, some commentators, anxious to preserve a faulty understanding of God's grace, attempt to convince us that the "outer darkness" to which Jesus was referring is not hell. Rather, they claim that it is a reference to the alleged "outer fringes of heaven." There, unfaithful believers will purportedly weep and gnash their teeth in regret, realizing how their reward could have been so much greater had they been obedient. Some who espouse this particular theory even go so far as to claim that the weeping of those unfaithful saints will only be temporary, because Jesus "will wipe every tear from their eyes" and then release them from heaven's outer darkness to join those "on the inside."

If, however, we study every other instance in Matthew's Gospel where Jesus spoke of "outer darkness" and "weeping and gnashing of teeth," (see Matt. 8:12; 13:42, 50; 22:13; 24:51), it becomes obvious that He was referring to hell and not to a place supposedly found in the "outer fringes" of heaven. Consider, for example, Jesus' explanation of His Parable of the Wheat and the Tares:

> So just as the tares are gathered up and burned with fire, so shall it be at the end of the age. The Son of Man will send forth His angels, and they will gather out of His kingdom

all stumbling blocks, and those who commit lawlessness, and will throw them *into the furnace of fire; in that place there will be weeping and gnashing of teeth.* Then the righteous will shine forth as the sun in the kingdom of their Father (Matt. 13:41-43, emphasis added).

Note that the damned will weep and gnash their teeth in "the furnace of fire," a clear reference to hell. Are we to believe that some of the righteous in heaven (in the alleged "outer fringes") will react identically to the damned, weeping and gnashing their teeth? It would be just as logical to conclude—when we read scriptures about deceased people rejoicing and praising God—that we are reading about people in the "outer fringes" of hell who are glad that they aren't in the deeper domains of torment!

Consider also Jesus' Parable of the Dragnet:

Again, the kingdom of heaven is like a dragnet cast into the sea, and gathering fish of every kind; and when it was filled, they drew it up on the beach; and they sat down and gathered the good fish into containers, but the bad they threw away. So it will be at the end of the age; the angels will come forth and take out the wicked from among the righteous, and will throw *them into the furnace of fire; in that place there will be weeping and gnashing of teeth* (Matt. 13:47-50, emphasis added).

Those who claim that the outer darkness mentioned by Jesus in His Parable of the Talents is a place in heaven might as well also claim that the "furnace of fire" mentioned by Jesus in His Parable of the Dragnet is also a place in heaven, because people there weep and gnash their teeth just as do those in the "outer darkness."

Moreover, does Jesus want us to believe that a person can be

judged by an angry God as being "wicked" and "worthless"—
as was the unfaithful servant in His Parable of the Talents—and
still be a heaven-bound child of God who is safe in His grace?
That same Jesus, in His Parable of the Dragnet, spoke of the
"wicked" being cast into the "furnace of fire."

Another Unfaithful Servant

Let's consider just one more "weeping and gnashing of teeth"
passage. At the same time and before the same audience to
whom He told His Parable of the Talents, Jesus spoke about another unfaithful servant:

> Who then is the faithful and sensible slave whom his mas-
> ter put in charge of his household to give them their food
> at the proper time? Blessed is that slave whom his master
> finds so doing when he comes. Truly I say to you that he will
> put him in charge of all his possessions. But if that evil slave
> says in his heart, "My master is not coming for a long time,"
> and begins to beat his fellow slaves and eat and drink with
> drunkards; the master of that slave will come on a day when
> he does not expect him and at an hour which he does not
> know, and will cut him in pieces and assign him a place with
> the hypocrites; in that place *there will be weeping and gnashing
> of teeth* (Matt. 24:45-51, emphasis added).

Was Jesus trying to communicate that the unfaithful servant
ultimately went to heaven, or to heaven's "outer fringes"? Surely not. Scripture solemnly warns that the litmus test of authentic
salvation is one's love for God's servants (see 1 John 3:10, 14;
4:7-8, 20), yet the unfaithful slave was found beating his fellow slaves. Scripture also declares that no drunkard will inherit
God's kingdom (see 1 Cor. 6:9-10), yet the unfaithful slave was
eating and drinking with drunkards. We read that the unfaith-

ful servant was ultimately "cut in pieces" and assigned "a place with the hypocrites" where "there will be weeping and gnashing their teeth." Clearly, that is hell.

All of this is to say that the unfaithful, wicked and worthless slave in Jesus' Parable of the Talents ended up in hell, *and the reason is because he brought no return on his master's investment*. If he would have only invested his single talent in the bank and gained some interest, that apparently could have saved him. But he buried his talent in the ground.

More Theological Wiggling

Because it is logically undeniable that the unfaithful servant in Jesus' Parable of the Talents was cast into hell, some commentators claim that the third servant represents someone who was never born again, and the single talent that he received and buried represents his God-given opportunity to hear and believe the gospel, which he rejected.

Although it could be true that the unfaithful servant represents a person who was never saved, there is a major problem with that interpretation as well—the problem of context. When Jesus told His Parable of the Talents, He was speaking to a few of His closest, most devoted disciples. In Mark's Gospel, they are listed as being Peter, James, John and Andrew (see Mark 13:3). Sitting on the Mount of Olives, they had asked Jesus some questions about the destruction of the Jerusalem temple and of His coming. His response is recorded in Matthew chapters 24 and 25, what is known as the Olivet Discourse.

Within that discourse, Jesus repeatedly emphasized to those few disciples the importance of *their* being ready when He returned (see Matt. 24:33, 42, 44; 25:13). In fact, the importance of them being ready could be considered to be His primary theme throughout the entire discourse.

In order to be ready, they needed to be found doing His will

when He returned. He underscored the importance of that by
first telling them about an unfaithful servant who ended up in
hell because he was not prepared for his master's return (see
Matt. 24:45-51). Remember, He told *them* about the unfaithful
servant to motivate *them* to be ready.

He then told them about five virgins who were refused en-
trance to a wedding feast because they were unprepared when
the delayed bridegroom appeared (see Matt. 25:1-13). He ended that parable by telling Peter, Andrew, James and John, "Be
on the alert then, for *you* do not know the day nor the hour"
(Matt. 25:13, emphasis added). That is, "Peter, Andrew, James
and John, don't be like the five foolish virgins." Clearly, Jesus
believed the possibility existed for them to become like the five
foolish virgins; otherwise He would not have warned them.

Then He told them the Parable of the Talents, a story about yet
another servant who went to hell because he was unprepared
for his master's return (see Matt. 25:14-30). Again, Jesus told
them that parable to motivate *them* to be ready.

> **The goats will
> discover to their
> horror that they
> are unprepared
> to stand before
> the Lord
> because of their
> poor stewardship.**

Finally, He told those few from
among His most devoted disciples about the future judgment
of the sheep and the goats, when
the goats will discover to their
horror that they are unprepared
to stand before the Lord because
of their poor stewardship. They
will consequently be cast into hell
(see Matt. 25:31-46). Again, Jesus
told some of *His disciples* about
that future judgment to motivate
them to be ready.

Although Peter, Andrew, James and John may have later told
unsaved people about Jesus' warnings and of the consequences

of not being ready, there isn't any doubt that they understood that His words applied primarily to themselves (and to any followers of Christ who want to make sure they are ready when He returns). All of them knew that they could potentially make the same error as the unfaithful servant. Like him, they could miscalculate their master's return, backslide, be unprepared, and share his fate. Any of them could become like the five foolish virgins, who were initially prepared for the bridegroom's coming but became unprepared, and who consequently were locked out of the wedding feast. Any of them could become like the goats if they ignored the pressing needs of the "least of these" (Matt. 25:45). And any of them could become like the unfaithful servant who buried his talent, and who consequently was cast into hell.

I encourage you to read all of Matthew 24 and 25 to convince yourself that what I am saying is undeniably true.[1] How tragic it is that these clear facts are ignored or denied by so many professing Christians who have turned "the grace of our God into licentiousness" (Jude 4), a heresy that is as old as the New Testament.

Suffice it to say that, after hearing Jesus' clear warnings, Peter, Andrew, James and John—who were certainly saved, heaven-bound individuals when He spoke to them that day on the Mount of Olives—all understood that they could potentially forfeit salvation and be cast into hell if they were poor stewards of their time, talents and treasures.

---

[1] Here is a more thorough list of scriptures that all indicate or imply that it is possible for a genuine Christian to forfeit salvation either by abandoning faith or by returning to the practice of sin: Matt. 18:21-35; 24:4-5, 11-13, 23-26, 42-51; 25:1-30; Luke 8:11-15; 11:24-26; 12:42-46; John 6:66-71; 8:31-32, 51; 15:1-6; Acts 11:21-23; 14:21-22; Rom. 6:11-23; 8:12-14, 17; 11:20-22; 1 Cor. 9:23-27; 10:1-21; 11:29-32; 15:1-2; 2 Cor. 1:24; 11:2-4; 12:21-13:5; Gal. 5:1-4; 6:7-9; Phil. 2:12-16; 3:17-4:1; Col. 1:21-23; 2:4-8, 18-19; 1 Thes. 3:1-8; 1 Tim. 1:3-7, 18-20; 4:1-16; 5:5-6, 11-15, 6:9-12, 17-19, 20-21; 2 Tim. 2:11-18; 3:13-15; Heb. 2:1-3; 3:6-19; 4:1-16: 5:8-9; 6:4-9, 10-20; 10:19-39; 12:1-17, 25-29; Jas. 1:12-16; 4:4-10; 5:19-20; 2 Pet. 1:5-11; 2:1-22; 3:16-17; 1 John 2:15-2:28; 5:16; 2 John 6-9; Jude 20-21; Rev. 2:7, 10-11, 17-26; 3:4-5, 8-12, 14-22; 21:7-8; 22:18-19

And if that was true for them, who among us can claim that it is not also true for us? Thus we see the grave consequences of poor stewardship.

Again, many professing Christians scoff at any theology that affirms the biblical truth that faith without works is dead, useless and cannot save (see Jas. 2:14-24), or that God's grace does not mitigate the necessity of holiness, but rather instructs "us to deny ungodliness and worldly desires and to live sensibly, righteously and godly in the present age" (Titus 2:11-12). Like the goats Jesus spoke of in His foretelling of the judgment of the sheep and goats, they will be shocked when they stand before Him and are condemned by the One whom they thought was their Savior.

And that brings me back to my original thought. Jesus is like a venture capitalist. Yet the rewards for doing well with what He has entrusted to us are much greater than any earthly venture capitalist could offer. Similarly, the consequences for not bringing some return to Him are potentially much more severe than what one would experience dealing with any earthly venture capitalist.

The Bible repeatedly teaches us that God endeavors to motivate people through rewards and punishments, and the Parable of the Talents emphasizes both. Wise readers will take note and determine to please the One who "is a rewarder of them that diligently seek Him" (Heb. 11:6b, KJV). Then, we don't have to fear punishment, but can look forward to rewards.

The First Lesson

This is the foundation for becoming *forever rich:* God is the owner of everything. He entrusts some of His wealth to each of us. One day we will each have to give an account of our stewardship and be proportionately rewarded or punished. We want to avoid punishment at all costs and pursue the greatest rewards.

If we embrace those truths, it will be reflected in our actions and lifestyles. Our belief will then become a basis for diligence, thrift, contentment, integrity, investment, sacrifice and generosity, all subjects of later chapters.

CHAPTER TWO
You've Won the Lottery

They are the envy of everyone, born among a very privileged class, living lives that most others can only dream of. Because they are so wealthy, they never give even a fleeting thought to lacking anything they truly need. In fact, they own so much more than they need that they have trouble finding room to store all their possessions. To that end, they often discard what the average person would love to possess. And because they associate only with others who are as wealthy as them, they are generally oblivious to the teeming majority of people who live at an unimaginably lower standard.

Who are these very fortunate people?

They are you, your family, your friends, and your neighbors.

Most of us have no idea how wealthy we are compared to most of the world's people. Let me see if I can help with some perspective.

One way to measure your wealth is to subtract your debts from the value of everything you own—your clothing, furniture, appliances, cars, home and so on. That gives you your net worth. Here is an astounding fact: If your net worth is $2,200 or more, you are in the top half of the world's wealthiest people.[1] To be among the richest 10 percent of adults in the world, all you need is a net worth of $61,000.[2]

---

[1] See http://articles.moneycentral.msn.com/News/StudyRevealsOverwhelmingWealth-Gap.aspx

[2] At this writing in 2011, the median net worth for people ages 45 to 54 in the United States

Another way to measure your wealth is by your income. Over 80 percent of the world's people live on less than $10 per day. That is less than $3,650 per year. Over 50 percent of the world's people live on less than $2.50 per day. That is less than $913 per year. Around 20 percent of the world's people live on less than $1.25 per day. That is less than $457 per year.[3]

Those whose incomes put them in the bottom 10 percent of the U.S. population are still better off than two-thirds of the world's population.[4]

If you would like to know your personal global ranking, navigate on your computer (an item owned by a minority of people) to www.globalrichlist.com. Select your currency, type in your annual income, and you will immediately know where you stand in comparison to the rest of the world. An annual income of $34,000 puts you in the top 5 percent. An annual income of $47,500 puts you in the world's top 1 percent.

It might also help us to remember that about nine million people will die of hunger this year. 24,447 will die of hunger *today*. Nearly one *billion* people are presently undernourished. That is about 1 in 7 of the world's people.[5] 1.4 *billion* people do not have access to safe drinking water. That's 1 in 5 of the world's people.

Born with the Silver Spoon

It's as if we've won the lottery, or were born into royalty. So much of our wealth is simply due to the fact that we've been born in the right place.

---

was $98,350 per person. To see the mean net worth for your age group, see http://cgi.money.cnn.com/tools/networth_ageincome/index.html

[3] See www.globalissues.org/article/26/poverty-facts-and-stats#src1

[4] See http://en.wikipedia.org/wiki/International_inequality

[5] These statistics can be found from many sources. For a real-time update, see www.stopthehunger.com

Warren Buffett, currently one of the world's wealthiest people, freely admits this very thing, stating, "If you stick me down in the middle of Bangladesh or Peru, you'll find out how much this talent is going to produce in the wrong kind of soil." Like Buffet, if you or I had been born in Bangladesh, chances are very good that we would be very poor. Compared to the rest of the world, it's like we're living in Disneyland.

> **Compared to the rest of the world, it's like we're living in Disneyland.**

My intention in writing this is not to make anyone feel guilty about being born in a wealthy nation or about his or her annual income. You had no choice regarding where you were born, and there is nothing wrong with earning money, as long as God is not dishonored through the means. My hope, however, is that you will begin to understand how wealthy you already are. How blessed is that day when you realize you've been living on an island of fantasy in an ocean of reality. Only then might you grasp the second secret to being forever rich, which is to *learn contentment*. If you can learn to be content, you can potentially lay up much more treasure in heaven.

Learning to be content requires real effort, because formidable forces are at work to make us discontent. Western culture is materialistic—to the maximum. Everyone is striving for more "stuff," and we are continually bombarded with advertisements designed to make us dissatisfied with what we currently have—in order to persuade us to make a purchase. The people in the commercials are always smiling, and surely we could be happy too if we just had what those happy people have.

The Ad Men At It

Think of what a difficult task automobile advertisers face. They know that most everyone who views their commercials already owns a car that takes them everywhere they want to go. They also know that most of those automobile owners purchased their existing cars by trading months (and in some cases, years) of their lives in daily labor to earn the money they need to make payments on a depreciating asset. Yet those advertisers hope to persuade such people to trade in their existing cars, go deeper into debt, and pledge many more months of daily labor to pay off their new debt—just so they can own a car that does almost exactly what their current car does! The advertisers' only hope of success is if they can somehow make us discontent.

And so they do. The cars in their ads are driven by good-looking people, and the subliminal message is that you can improve your sex appeal and intelligence if you drive their make and model. If there are children in the backseat, they are also attractive and well behaved, sending a message that this car will also improve your children. Such cars are always driven on scenic roads along the ocean, through well-manicured suburbs, or past posh city skyscrapers, telling you that your life can also be upgraded. And they never need to be washed because they're never dirty. Most importantly, you can be sure that others will admire you if you drive the car in the commercial. Even if you don't own a second home in the mountains, an SUV can at least lead people to believe that you might. As you drive by, they'll imagine you four-wheeling across wilderness streams to reach your hideaway cabin!

> **The advertisers' only hope of success is if they can somehow make us discontent.**

Let's face it. Most of us don't buy cars to take us from Point A to Point B. We purchase cars to make a statement about ourselves as we drive between Points A and B.

If we can just learn to be more content, however, we could keep our cars longer without embarrassment. We might even start purchasing pre-owned cars, saving ourselves tens of thousands of dollars in the years ahead, which will make it possible to lay up even more riches in heaven.

Let me tell you one of the greatest blessings of owning an older car, especially one that has some dings and dents: When you walk out of Wal-mart and discover that the person who parked beside you opened his door carelessly and put another ding in your door, it doesn't ruin your day. It's just another ding! Life goes on. Compare that with the discovery of the very first ding on your just-purchased, showroom shiny, 48-future-payments-to-go automotive idol…

The Joy of Contentment

The honest truth is that none of us need anything more than what we currently own. In fact, we could get by on much less if we were so motivated. As soon as we shift into contentment, a huge weight rolls off of our shoulders, and the future becomes instantly brighter.

Think about this: If unhappiness stems from unfulfilled desires, then there are only two roads to happiness, either by (1) fulfilling or (2) abandoning those unfulfilled desires. The latter generates instant happiness. The former often produces protracted unhappiness as the unhappy person strives to fulfill a desire that may never be fulfilled. And how many unhappy people, if they do fulfill a desire, discover it to be empty and… *unfulfilling*? At that point, some learn the lesson, but many remain tragically deceived and simply reset their discontentment to focus on yet another acquisition. Such people are trading the certain happiness that accompanies contentment for just a chance of future, fleeting happiness. We are wise, then, to heed the wisdom of G.K. Chesterson: "There are two ways to get enough. One is to continue to accumulate more and more. The other is to desire less."

But aren't people who are contented purposeless and lazy? Isn't it the discontented who dream of better things and thus make progress and achieve?

The answer is yes and no. People who are *completely* content are indeed sometimes purposeless and lazy. I'm not advocating, however, the abandonment of all unfulfilled desires. Scripture only advocates abandoning misguided desires, which includes seeking happiness in the acquisition of more earthly, material things. That, in a nutshell, is what Jesus was prescribing when He told His followers to lay up treasures in heaven rather than on earth. He meant for them to abandon one desire for a better, more worthy desire. Obeying Him in that regard requires being both content and discontent—content with what one has on earth and discontent with what one has in heaven.

Again, most of us already have more than enough on earth due to misguided desires. We've been foolish, pursuing temporal, earthly happiness, rather than eternal, heavenly happiness. We've been building sandcastles at low tide.

The Gain of Contentment

Writing to Timothy, the apostle Paul penned important words about the great value of contentment:

> ....men of depraved mind and deprived of the truth, who suppose that godliness is a means of gain. But godliness actually is a means of great gain when accompanied by contentment. For we have brought nothing into the world, so we cannot take anything out of it either. If we have food and covering, with these we shall be content. But those who want to get rich fall into temptation and a snare and many foolish and harmful desires which plunge men into ruin and destruction. For the love of money is a root of all sorts of evil, and some by longing for it have wandered away

from the faith and pierced themselves with many griefs. But flee from these things, you man of God (1 Tim. 6:5b-11a).

Note that Paul first condemned those whose minds were "depraved" by reason of their thinking that "godliness is a means of gain" (1 Tim. 6:5). In light of his next few sentences, it is obvious that the gain he was referring to was earthly, material gain.

However, lest Timothy think he believed that there was *no* advantage to living a godly life, Paul qualified his condemnation by adding, "But godliness actually is a means of great gain when accompanied by contentment" (1 Tim. 6:6). So, living obediently to God's commandments is actually very profitable as long as the obedient person is content, which indicates that payday doesn't come immediately.

So when does payday come? Paul's next sentences bring it all together: "For we have brought nothing into the world, so we cannot take anything out of it either. If we have food and covering, with these we shall be content" (1 Tim. 6:7-8). Clearly, payday is in the next life. We can't take anything with us when we leave this world, so it is foolish to pile up earthly treasures. We can, however, send those treasures ahead of us to heaven. Thus it makes perfect sense to learn to be content with as little as possible now, even if it amounts to nothing more than our most basic necessities of food and covering.

> **We can't take anything with us when we leave this world, so it is foolish to pile up earthly treasures.**

Paul's words are certainly convicting. How can we claim that we would be content with just food and covering if we're not content with all that we currently do possess, which is so much more than food and covering?

The Danger of Discontentment

Discontentment drives us to foolishly acquire and cling to what we don't really need and what we ultimately won't own. Worse, according to Paul as he continued admonishing Timothy, discontentment drives some into "ruin and destruction." Read his words again:

> Those who want to get rich fall into temptation and a snare and many foolish and harmful desires which plunge men into ruin and destruction. For the love of money is a root of all sorts of evil, and some by longing for it have wandered away from the faith and pierced themselves with many griefs (1 Tim. 6:9-10).

Discontentment/longing for money is so dangerous that, if not checked, can cause believers to "wander away from the faith" according to Paul. To wander away from the faith is to wander away from what is required for ultimate salvation.

We need to be content with what we already possess.

Paul's warning against being among those who "want to get rich" makes me wonder how his words should be applied to people like me and you, people who already are rich. We are magnificently wealthy compared to his contemporary readers, not to mention most of the people in today's world. We own material possessions that people in Paul's day couldn't have even dreamed of owning, like automobiles and computers. Most people in today's world can't afford those things. So how do Paul's words apply to us?

Certainly, at bare minimum, we need to be content with what we already possess and carefully consider the necessity of any additional acquisitions, knowing that we have the same two choices as Paul's contemporary readers. We can lay up our treasures on earth temporarily, understanding that our ownership ends at death, or we can lay them up in heaven and enjoy "great gain" eternally.

Additionally, we can consider scaling down in order to transfer assets from earth to heaven, which is the topic of a later chapter, so I won't elaborate on it now.

Words to the Rich

In the very same chapter of 1 Timothy from which we've been reading, Paul did have some special words to those who were rich in his day that can help very rich folks like us today:

> Instruct those who are rich in this present world not to be conceited or to fix their hope on the uncertainty of riches, but on God, who richly supplies us with all things to enjoy. Instruct them to do good, to be rich in good works, to be generous and ready to share, storing up for themselves the treasure of a good foundation for the future, so that they may take hold of that which is life indeed (1 Tim. 6:17-19).

First, take note that Paul refers to us rich folks as being "rich in this present world," underscoring the fact that folks like us may not be rich in the world to come.

Second, Paul warns us against being prideful because of our wealth. Pride is certainly a temptation that stalks the wealthy. To succumb to pride's temptation is to forget that God is the source of our wealth. How wealthy would you be had you been born to a prostitute in Calcutta?

Third, Paul reminds us that riches are uncertain. One of the richest people who ever lived once wrote, "Do not weary yourself to gain wealth, cease from your consideration of it.

When you set your eyes on it, it is gone. For wealth certainly makes itself wings like an eagle that flies toward the heavens" (Prov. 23:4-5).

Our hopes for a favorable future should be set on God alone, the One who, as Paul wrote, "richly supplies us with all things to enjoy" (1 Tim. 6:17). I like those words. God created the material world, and when He did, He saw that it was all "very good" (Gen. 1:31). He has abundantly provided us with enjoyable things. Keep in mind, however, that many of those enjoyable things He provides are life's simple pleasures. When you hold your grandchild, savor a sunrise, or eat a crisp, sweet apple, you know God loves you.

Fourth, Paul admonishes us to use our God-given resources "to do good, to be rich in good works, to be generous and ready to share" (1 Tim. 6:18). Our lives should be characterized by liberal sharing that is proportionate to God's blessings upon us. And why? So that we might store up for ourselves "the treasure of a good foundation for the future" (1 Tim. 6:19). That is, that we might lay up treasure in heaven.

> **It is those who are the wealthiest who are often the least content.**

Finally, Paul promises that so doing will result in our "taking hold of that which is life indeed" (1 Tim. 6:19). Although selfish, indulgent, rich people may think their lives are wonderful, they have not taken hold of true life, that is, life as God intended, now and forever. Jesus declared, "Whoever loses his life for My sake will find it" (Matt. 16:25). True and eternal life is found in giving up one's life, trading selfishness for unselfishness, loving God and neighbor. Thus, learning contentment is essential, as discontentment breeds selfishness.

Surely the more one possesses, the more he ought to be contented, but such is often not the case. In fact, it is those who are the wealthiest who are often the least content, as they are driven by the deception that happiness is found in more stuff.

Back to the Beginning

Let's conclude this chapter by going back to where we started, thinking about how rich we already are.

Consider Adam and Eve. When they were created, they didn't have any "stuff." All they possessed was a relationship with God, a relationship with each other, and an opportunity to enjoy a marvelous, pristine creation. So were they poor and to be pitied in their God-given state?

They owned nothing, but lived in a paradise.

Should we have expected to find them downcast in their deep "poverty"? I don't think so. They owned nothing, but lived in a paradise.

Surely the initial God-created state of Adam and Eve serves as a divine commentary on what is *truly* valuable. Therefore, if I have a genuine relationship with God and possess a loving relationship with just one other human being, and if I can see the stars in the sky, smell the fragrance of flowers, hear the singing of birds, taste the sweetness of watermelon, and feel a cool breeze on a sultry day, I am rich—as rich as Adam and Eve. I have every reason to be joyfully content.

Most readers will have to admit that they have much more than Adam and Eve. We have a relationship with God through our Lord Jesus. We have not just one, but many loving relationships with other human beings. God's creation is as marvelous as it has always been. And we are far wealthier than Adam and Eve were! So we are faced with a choice. We can either be discontented and use our wealth to acquire more stuff for ourselves, or we can be content, using our wealth to love more people—particularly those who are lacking the most basic necessities. Choosing the latter, we demonstrate our love for God, enriching our relationship with Him.

In doing that, we become truly rich and *forever rich*.

You say, "If I had a little more, I should be very satisfied." You make a mistake. If you are not content with what you have, you would not be satisfied if it were doubled.
— Charles H. Spurgeon

Make sure that your character is free from the love of money, being content with what you have; for He Himself has said, "I will never desert you, nor will I ever forsake you" (Heb. 13:5).

CHAPTER THREE
Scaling Down in Disneyland

Although Jesus commanded it and the early Christians did it, I'd be willing to bet that you've never heard a single sermon on it. I'm speaking of self-dispossession. To self-dispossess is to divest yourself of something that you own.

Most Christians know that Jesus told the rich young ruler to sell his possessions and give the proceeds to charity, but those same Christians are often quick to say that was a special incident. Jesus only ever told one man to sell his possessions, they claim. The truth, however, is that Jesus commanded all of His followers to sell their possessions and give to charity:

> And He said to His disciples…. "Sell your possessions and give to charity; make yourselves money belts which do not wear out, an unfailing treasure in heaven, where no thief comes near nor moth destroys. For where your treasure is, there your heart will be also" (Luke 12:22, 33-34).

Take note that Jesus' intention was not to impoverish His followers through their self-dispossession. His intention was to *enrich* them—*forever*. He really wasn't advocating self-dispossession, but rather, wise relocation of wealth, from earth to heaven. He advocated the same for the rich young ruler. Jesus wanted to save him from the inevitable loss of all his wealth. He wanted him to transfer it to heaven where it would be safe forever.

Jesus wants to save rich people like you and me from the same folly. Remember, "He is no fool who gives up what he cannot keep to gain what he cannot lose."

The Right Stuff

If someone who is not wealthy (on earth) desires to be wealthy, generally three things are necessary for him to reach his goal: sacrifice, diligence and saving. The same is true for those who want to be *forever rich*. Sacrifice, diligence and saving (in heaven) are required.

It is also often true that those who desire to become rich on earth practice some form of self-dispossession in order to reach their goal. Perhaps they sell assets in order to have sufficient capital to start a business or make an investment, effectively transferring wealth from one form to another, risking money in hopes of gaining more. Or perhaps they borrow—which is a dispossession of some of their future income and another form of transferring wealth from one form to another—with the hope of gaining more.

In the same way, the one who desires to become *forever rich* must also transfer wealth from one form to another. Yet he takes no risk whatsoever. His investment cannot fail because God guarantees it. He only needs to be content as he waits for the day to enjoy it. But like anyone who hopes to become rich on earth, he must practice the principle of "delayed gratification." That is, he gives up present enjoyment to gain future enjoyment, which is the opposite of "instant gratification." Storing up heavenly treasure is all about delayed gratification.

There is a video on YouTube that wonderfully illustrates the struggles of delayed gratification. (You can see it for yourself by searching on YouTube for "the marshmallow test.") Young children are seated alone in a room, and a marshmallow is placed on a table in front of them. The children are told that they can eat the marshmallow immediately if they desire.

However, if they would like to eat not one, but two marsh-mallows, they must wait to be brought a second marshmallow without eating the first one. It is very easy to identify with the children in the video as they wait for their benefactor to return while they stare at the single marshmallow before them, touching and smelling it, and sometimes taking tiny nibbles. They each do their best to delay their gratification. One blond-haired little girl takes so many tiny nibbles as she waits that her marsh-mallow shrinks to half its original size.[1]

If Jesus expected His earliest followers—the large majority of whom were quite poor compared to most of us—to delay their gratification and divest themselves of their possessions in order to lay up heavenly treasures, it would seem reasonable to think that He expects no less from us. In fact, because "to whom much is given much is required," it would seem reasonable to think that He would expect more from us.

That being so, we should all ask ourselves, "How have I obeyed Jesus' commandment concerning self-dispossession? What have I sold, using the proceeds to lay up heavenly trea-sure?"

Self-Deceptions that Prevent Self-Dispossession

Unfortunately, too many professing Christians are fooling themselves with their answers to those questions. Some will claim that they've fulfilled Jesus' commandment through "in-ward relinquishment." That is, they've given all their posses-sions to Christ "in their hearts" while giving up nothing in real-ity. So all that they now own supposedly belongs to Jesus—even

---

[1] When the original "marshmallow experiment" was conducted decades ago, researchers at Stanford followed up on the children as they grew older and discovered those who delayed their gratification were more likely to do well in school, achieve higher SAT scores, and obtain better jobs as adults. Those children who did poorly in the marshmallow experiment were more likely to be overweight, have drug problems, and be generally less successful in life.

though it is just as much in their possession as it was before they "gave it all to Jesus."

This kind of self-deception is rooted in the idea that God is mostly concerned with heart attitudes rather than outward actions—as if the two are unrelated. It is often expressed in common sayings, such as, "God looks only at our hearts, not at what we possess."

This line of reasoning stands in direct opposition to what Jesus taught. Remember, when He told His followers not to lay up treasures on earth but in heaven, He concluded with the words, "For where your treasure is, there your heart will be also" (Luke 12:34). That is, where we put our treasures, either in heaven or on earth, reveals where our hearts are. *Our actions reveal what is in our hearts.* So it is simply not true that God looks only at our hearts and not at what we possess. Rather, when He looks at what we possess, He knows what is in our hearts. We may fool ourselves, but we can't fool Him.

> ## Our actions reveal what is in our hearts.

Such is the case of the person who has "internally relinquished" all of his possessions to Jesus. It would be interesting to see what would happen if I used that method of relinquishment when paying my taxes. When an IRS agent comes knocking at my door, I'll just tell him, "I've internally paid my taxes, and in my heart I've given you all that I owe you." I suspect that IRS agent would quickly conclude that my failure to actually pay my taxes is a sure indication that in my heart I don't want to pay my taxes. God is no dummy either!

Simple and honest logic alone should be enough to convince us that it is our actions that reveal what is truly in our hearts. What would we think of the person who, as he stabs a knife into his victim's back, says, "I really don't hate this person whom I'm stabbing…inwardly, I'm full of love"? Or how about a person

whose house is stacked to the ceiling with pornographic magazines and who says, "These magazines mean nothing to me…in-
wardly, I'm pure"? Or how about a drunk person who says with
a slur, "Inwardly, I'm sober"? Surely in every case we would
consider these people to be sadly self-deceived. Their actions
reveal their hearts while their words reveal their self-deception.
Then why do we fool ourselves about our possessions and say,
"All of these possessions mean nothing to me…they all belong
to Jesus"? If they mean nothing, why are we clinging to them?
Why are we ignoring what Jesus said regarding them?

Here is another common Christian cliché that reveals a self-
deception regarding the connection between actions and heart
attitudes: "It doesn't matter what you possess as long as you
hold it loosely." That is doublespeak, a declaration that it is OK
to be unwilling to give as long as you are willing to give. An unwilling willingness! The one who is holding something loosely
is still holding it. His treasure is still on the earth. His actions
reveal his heart.

Here's yet another statement that reveals the same self-deception: "If the Lord told me to give away any of my possessions, I
would do it in a second." Such a person imagines that his heart
is right and that he is willing to relinquish anything that the
Lord would require of him. Yet, as we just read in Luke 12:33-34,
Jesus has commanded all of His disciples to sell their possessions, give to charity and lay up treasure in heaven. So the person who imagines he is willing to give up his possessions proves
that he is actually unwilling by his ignoring Christ's clear commandment. It could be said that he is doubly deceived, as he
imagines that what Christ required of all of His disciples is not
required of him, and he imagines that if it ever is required, he
will surely obey.

One final indication of the same kind of self-deception is the
alteration of Jesus' commandment from, "Do not lay up treasures on earth" to, "Do not treasure your earthly possessions."

That is, of course, a serious perversion of what Jesus said and meant. Adjusting only our attitudes about our possessions will not prevent thieves from stealing them or rust from consuming them. Only by actually selling our possessions and laying them up in heaven do we prevent their inevitable demise.

Let us not be deceived!

First Steps

When you first begin to consider self-dispossession, you may well discover, as I did, inward resistance to the whole idea. That is a depressing yet glorious moment, because you then begin to realize how much all your stuff means to you...and how much of your heart is on the earth with all your treasures. At that moment of self-realization, a war begins. It can be misery at first, but with each step of obedience, your joy increases as you prove your love for Jesus.

Many begin by selling only the possessions that they never use or enjoy, as those are the easiest to let go. We advertise a garage sale and unload all the junk in our attics and garages and then give the money to some worthy cause. That is a start, of course. The Holy Spirit, however, who indwells all true believers to help them be holy, will help you to think about ways to lay up even more treasure in heaven.

For example, the Spirit might help you to see, as He did me, that you could sell your house and use the equity to purchase a smaller house without debt (or less debt), which could enable you to lay up tens of thousands of dollars in heaven in the years ahead.

He might help you realize that you could stop buying a new car every year and buy one every eight years—or never buy another new car and always buy a used one—again enabling you to lay up tens of thousands of dollars in heaven during the rest of your life.

He might help you to unload those luxuries that serve no other purpose than to impress other people, swell your ego, or indulge your flesh. Diamonds, for example, are in this category (but don't expect to sell them for anywhere close to what you paid for them…a good lesson in lousy earthly investments).

Here's another possibility: The Spirit might help you to make a decision to delay your retirement (or never retire), thus eliminating the need for storing up so much earthly treasure in retirement savings, enabling the storing up of hundreds of thousands of dollars in heaven, waiting for your *eternal* retirement.

> **The important thing is to look at our homes, as well as every other material possession, in the light of God's eternal kingdom and use it accordingly.**

Please note that I've written in the preceding paragraphs about what the Holy Spirit *might* lead you to do, because everyone's circumstances are different. God may be leading you not to scale down to a smaller house, but to purchase a larger one—if it is for some kingdom purpose such as adopting orphans from another country, raising a big tribe of radical disciples, or facilitating church gatherings. One who does that is just as effectively "giving up his house for Christ" as the one who sells his large home, buys a smaller one, and gives the remaining equity to the poor. The important thing is to look at our homes, as well as every other material possession, in the light of God's eternal kingdom and use it accordingly.

Here is yet another consideration regarding what is the average person's most valuable possession: Sharing your home in some fashion can be a great means to lay up more treasure in heaven, either by freely giving room to a needy person or by renting part of your home to a not-so-needy person and giving the rental income to charity.

Jesus, of course, didn't lay down any specific commandments meant to regulate our possessions. For example, He never decreed the maximum allowable square footage of our homes or sticker prices of our cars. So we should be careful that we don't pass judgment on others in this regard. I know a few Christians—who are serious stewards of God's money—who need to drive fairly nice cars if they hope to do business with their upscale clientele. It is that business which makes it possible for those believers to meet many pressing needs of our spiritual family around the world each year—and lay up tons of treasure in heaven in the process.

To what degree should you scale down in Disneyland? I don't know the answer to that question. However, I am sure that, in heaven, none of us will regret any sacrifice that we made on earth for God's kingdom. There, having been fully dispossessed of every earthly treasure by death, we'll wish we had made greater sacrifices. We'll fully realize that we were foolish to not give up what we couldn't keep in order to gain what we could never lose. Thus, how wise it would be in this life for us to pray Moses' prayer: "Teach us to number our days, that we may present to You a heart of wisdom" (Psa. 90:12).

CHAPTER FOUR
Living Large on Less

Once you realize that your life is a journey to give an account before the Great Venture Capitalist, and once you've begun to understand how wealthy you are by comparison to most people in the world and learn contentment, and once you've started to obey Jesus' commandment of self-dispossession (which is actually just a prudent transfer of wealth from earth to heaven), life becomes much different. You begin to truly act like one who is a steward of what belongs to God, evaluating your financial decisions in light of the truth.

You probably will, as I have, wrestle over many decisions that relate to your stewardship. I have to admit that it hasn't been easy for me. My heart seems to still be at least partially on this earth. I live here, so like everyone else, I want to be happy here. Consequently, I need continual reminders that my earthly sojourn is infinitely short in comparison to my eternal future in the Kingdom of God.

In this chapter, I'd like to tell you something about my personal journey to living on less—including my struggles—in hopes that it will help you on your journey. Although I still have room to grow, I've made progress, and my wife and I are living on considerably less than what we lived on ten years ago, having significantly reduced our expenses to increase our heavenly investments. But it has been a journey that we've taken step by step.

The Debt Debate

One of the first light bulbs that switched on in our under-standing concerned debt. Debt can be a friend or foe. It can help or hinder you from laying up treasure in heaven.

Let's consider first how debt can actually be a blessing.

The ministry where I serve, *Heaven's Family*, works around the world to meet very pressing needs of the poorest of Christians, the "least of these" of whom Jesus spoke in His foretelling of the judgment of the sheep and the goats (see Matt. 25:31-46). We focus on helping believers who are facing even more daunting challenges than poverty, such as persecution, hunger, natural disasters, widowhood, illness, unsafe water, orphanhood and physical handicaps. We also establish micro-banks that provide small business startup loans to help enterprising believers lift themselves from poverty.

Through relatively small loans, very poor Christians who would otherwise not have had a chance to start their own busi-ness are empowered to become self-supporting and prosper. Their debts are temporary, and if you asked any of them if their indebtedness was a blessing or cursing, they would affirm the former. Their loans paved the way for a brighter future. As they've prospered, they've not only been empowered to meet their own needs, but also to meet the needs of others. They've been empowered to lay up treasures in heaven—through a loan.

Debt can be a blessing if it fosters prosperity that results in generosity. Without some kind of capital—either in the form of skills, knowledge, tools, or money—providing for oneself is virtually impossible. So borrowing money to gain marketable skills, knowledge, tools, raw materials, inventory, and so on, can be very wise, not only in developing nations, but in wealthier places.

Of course, when one borrows there is always risk, but without risk, there is no potential for reward. Therefore, all risks should be measured against their potential rewards. To borrow money, for example, to gain a college degree in a field that will likely be worthless in the marketplace is foolish. To borrow money, however, to gain an education that will provide an income for decades is wise.

Some Christians are opposed to any form of borrowing based on Paul's admonition, "Owe nothing to anyone except to love one another" (Rom. 13:8). If Paul was prohibiting all borrowing, however, we would have to wonder why he would contradict Jesus, who commanded His followers to compassionately lend, which would of course require assisting someone to commit the "sin" of borrowing (see Luke 6:35). We might also wonder why God similarly expected His people under the old covenant to compassionately lend to the poor among them, and also promised them that if they would obey His commandments, He would bless them so much that they would "lend to many nations" (Deut 15:6-8). Lending in either case would require helping others to borrow. And we also might wonder why Scripture says, "The wicked borrows and does not pay back" (Psa. 37:21), rather than "Only the wicked borrow."

Of course, Paul was not prohibiting all borrowing, but rather the sin of not repaying one's debts.

Foolish Borrowing

Borrowing money for depreciating assets is generally foolish as it results in having less and thus leads to poverty. For example, borrowing money to take a Caribbean cruise is a big mistake. Long after your tan has faded and you are back in your cubicle, you'll still be paying for something that only benefits people who are smarter than you—the investors in the credit card company who lent you their money. Credit card companies love stupid people, of which there is apparently no shortage.

I have a credit card, but I never charge more than I can pay off at the end of each month. If you don't have that kind of discipline, you need to perform some plastic surgery: Cut up your credit cards and pay only with cash.

If you have continual credit card debt, that is, *generally speaking*, an indication of discontentment, poor stewardship, and an ominous indicator of your riches-to-rags financial future. Credit card debt is generally the worst kind of debt because the cost of borrowing is so high. So as you set a goal to pay off all your debt, you should start with those debts that carry the highest interest rates. Those are usually credit card debts.

Getting out of debt requires self-discipline. The first step is to take an accounting of all your usual expenses. If you've been spending more than you've been taking in, there are only two possible solutions to your

Getting out of debt requires self-discipline.

problem. You can figure out some way to increase your income. Or you can do what you will be forced to do sooner or later, and that is figure out how to cut some of your expenses.

The reason I say that you will be forced to cut your expenses sooner or later is because it is inevitable. If you keep spending more than you take in, the only way to make up the difference is by borrowing. If you keep borrowing, your debt will keep growing. Eventually no one will lend you any more money, and you'll have to cut your expenses. So why wait until then when it will be all the more painful? Start doing it today. Start cutting out unnecessary expenses. No pain, no gain.

"But all my expenses are necessary!" some may cry.

Stop fooling yourself. *Billions* of people are living on less than you are. If you lost your source of income, you would immediately figure out ways to cut your expenses. You *can* reduce your expenses, live below your means, and get out of debt. Only then can you start laying up significant treasures in heaven in order to become *forever rich*.

The formula to get out of debt is really quite simple. Cut all unnecessary expenses. Use the money that was being wasted to pay off your credit cards, starting with the card that has the highest interest rate. Once you've paid off that credit card, you'll have additional money available each month to pay off the next credit card, and so on. Then pay off any other debts following the same principle—paying loans with the highest interest rates first. Your ability to pay your debts will snowball as each debt is paid off. If you stick with the program, you will eventually be debt free. No car payments, no house payments, no credit card debt! All the money that was being used to repay debt can then be used to lay up treasure in heaven.

My Journey

My wife and I made a decision years ago that we would only go into debt for cars, a house, and low-risk investments. However, after making eight years of car payments on two consecutive new cars, we decided to never again purchase a car on credit and to always purchase used cars. We've saved ourselves tens of thousands of dollars since then and have driven to all the same places that we would have driven had we purchased a new car on credit. The only thing we've deprived ourselves of is "the new car smell."

Most people feel richer when they drive their brand new car away from the dealership, but the truth is, they've instantly become several thousand dollars poorer, because their new car is immediately worth less than what they just paid for it. And if it was purchased on credit, they've made themselves poorer yet.

As I've previously mentioned, my wife and I also decided to sell our house and use the equity to purchase a less-expensive (but very adequate) house in order to more quickly eliminate all our debt. We went from a four-bedroom, three-bathroom, two-car garage mansion on ten country acres to a three-bedroom, one-bathroom, one-car garage mansion on one quarter of an acre in the suburbs. (I call them both mansions, because that is how the majority of people in the world would see them.) We've not only benefitted by owning our house debt-free, but our family of five has also grown in patience waiting in line for the bathroom. We're still living like kings. In fact, speaking of kings and bathrooms, Solomon, in all his glory, had no such luxury![1]

As we progressed on our journey, we realized that the only way we could lay up more treasure in heaven was either by increasing our income or decreasing our expenses. We didn't see much of way that we could increase our income, as that was derived from the ministry where we serve, and that ministry, by our own design, purposely keeps salaries and wages low in order to provide maximum resources to the "least of these" around the world.[2]

My wife, Becky, and I have occasionally toyed with moneymaking ideas, but we've always concluded (at least so far) that pursuing them would require time that we can't spare. So it doesn't seem likely that we'll be able to lay up more treasure in heaven by increasing our income in order to have more to give. That being so, our journey has focused primarily on finding ways to live on less. Besides making adjustments on housing and autos, we've also made some decisions regarding retirement savings.

---

[1] Is it better to buy or rent a residence? Generally speaking, buying on credit makes more sense than renting, as renters do not build equity in their residences, and they are likely paying off their landlord's mortgage. After thirty years of renting, renters have nothing to show for their 360 payments. Most borrowers, however, own their homes free and clear by then, and hopefully their homes will have increased in value to at least keep up with the rate of inflation. Yet there are other factors to take into consideration, as anyone will tell you who purchased a house that currently is worth less than what they paid for it. Beware of buying a home in a region where prices have recently appreciated significantly. What goes up quickly often comes down quickly.

[2] Most of us who work at *Heaven's Family* hope that the Lord is crediting us with some heavenly treasure for the difference between what we are currently paid and what we could earn using our skills elsewhere.

When we first began our journey, we liquidated most of the retirement savings we had accumulated and decided not to continuing saving, but to keep on working until we went to heaven. Also, as a minister, I had legally opted out of paying into Social Security when I was in my early twenties, which of course meant that we would never receive any Social Security retirement benefits. All of that is to say that we had nothing we could count on for retirement.

Last year, however, we reconsidered our decision and decided that, even though we still planned on serving in ministry as long as we could, there might come a time when one or both of us would not be able to keep working. (We are now in our early 50s.) So we decided to begin saving for that possibility, so that we would never be a burden to our children or anyone else. And if everything goes as we hope—that we will both be able to continue working until Jesus comes or He takes us home—then our modest retirement savings can ultimately be put to some other good use.

Please don't think that I am saying that you should necessarily follow my example. My situation is somewhat unique since I serve in vocational ministry. If I were doing any-

> When we stand before the Lord, we'll have to give an account for not only our treasures, but also our time.

thing else, I would probably be saving to retire at a reasonable age so that I would be free to spend my retirement serving the Lord, perhaps volunteering for some ministry.

One thing I would not be doing, however, is planning to retire so that I could live in self-indulgence. When we stand before the Lord, we'll have to give an account for not only our treasures, but also our time. I recommend that you spend your retirement being as fruitful as you can!

Other Decisions

Our next major decision concerned health insurance, which can be a very expensive item on a family's budget, and life insurance. Concerning health insurance, when I resigned by pastorate to launch the ministry of *Heaven's Family*, we simply couldn't afford health insurance, so we trusted the Lord. Eventually, however, we learned of a health insurance program offered by our state for low-income families that was funded by settlements from tobacco lawsuits. So, being poor by American standards (but rich), for as long as that program lasted we enjoyed excellent health insurance coverage for just $70 per month. Then we went back to having no health insurance. Now, *Heaven's Family* has an HRA (Health Reimbursement Account) plan for all its employees that reimburses us for healthcare expenses up to a set dollar amount.

Concerning life insurance, we cancelled my existing policy at the time. But a few years later I had second thoughts, especially

> "Each person must be fully convinced in his own mind" (Rom 14:5).

because I was doing so much travel to developing nations where anything could happen. Although I believe in God's protection, He has not promised that our persecutors will not kill us (or that I won't do something stupid). I decided that getting a life insurance policy would be an act of love towards my wife, so that her needs would be met in the event of my death (and I hoped that I wasn't giving her yet another reason to pray that the Lord would take me).

Again, don't think that I expect you to imitate my decisions. The point is, if you want to wisely transfer wealth from earth to heaven, you have to take some kind of action. Some readers might think I'm extreme, while others might think I've compromised. So "each person must be fully convinced in his own mind" (Rom 14:5).

Little Savings Add Up

There are so many other ways to cut expenses that seem less significant but that add up when done consistently over time. For example, you can clip coupons, be your children's barber, grow some of your own food, stop buying expensive foods and junk foods, and eat out less frequently. (It has been said, "To determine if you've been wasting money on food, just check your *wasteline*." Ouch!) You could adjust your thermostat, drive a smaller, more gas-efficient vehicle, keep that old furniture another five years, not replace the pet that died, avoid designer fashions, purchase clothing at thrift stores or when it is on sale and out-of-season, car-pool, take shorter showers, lower the thermostat on your hot water tank, go on more economical vacations, and so on. The list is endless.

Of course, frugality divorced from generosity is just frugality. The goal is not only to save money, but to save money that can be used to lay up more treasure in heaven.

Of course, saving money is not the only means of facilitating the laying up of treasure in heaven. Making more money is another means, a subject we'll explore next.

CHAPTER FIVE
Moola from Manure

It is, of course, impossible to lay up treasure in heaven unless you first have some treasure on earth to transfer. That is why we've been considering ways to eliminate debt and reduce expenses. We want to free up funds to deposit into our heavenly bank accounts.

Besides reducing expenses, the only other way to secure funds for heaven is by increasing income. If you can remain contented with your current standard of living, increasing your income can enable you to lay up in heaven 100 percent of that increase—as you demonstrate your love for the Lord and build His kingdom on earth. In such a case, earning money becomes pure ministry, just as much as anything else that can be labeled "ministry."

Let us not forget that there is nothing wrong with earning money, as long as the means of earning it are honorable before God. (You can't be a "prostitute for Jesus" as one woman actually claims who sells her body and donates much of her earnings to charity.) Earning money is virtuous when one's motive is to meet the needs of others. And when one gives a percentage of his earnings to lift the poor or extend God's kingdom, the effort spent to earn that percentage is 100 percent pure ministry.

God Calling

I think it is tragic that members of Christ's body are often spoken of as being divided into two categories, those who are "called to the ministry" and those who "do secular work." Both groups are called by God, and every member of Christ's body is called to ministry.

Just because God calls only some of His children to *vocational* ministry does not mean that those whom He doesn't call to vocational ministry are any less called to do what they do. If you ask, for example, any pastor or evangelist how he knew that God was calling him when he began to pursue vocational ministry, only a tiny minority will tell you about hearing God's audible voice or seeing a vision. The majority will simply tell you that they "felt led," realizing that God gave them the desire and gifts to serve Him in some vocational ministry. It comes down to the fact that they were interested and felt qualified, the same criteria that most people use to determine their career.

> **All of Christ's followers should seek His will regarding their specific vocational calling.**

God gifts people in different ways, and how He gifts them makes them more suited for some careers than others. And who can say that the gifting of the accountant, carpenter, homemaker, nurse or teacher is less of a gifting from God than the gifting of the pastor or evangelist?

Moreover, if it weren't for all those so-called "secular" giftings (which are actually all sacred), it would be impossible for anyone to pursue a calling to vocational ministry for the simple reason that the large majority of vocational ministers are sustained by those who earn money in "secular" jobs. To put it plainly, if everyone were called to vocational ministry, everyone would be starving.

All of this is to say that all of Christ's followers should seek His will regarding their specific vocational calling. And regardless of what it is that God calls us to do, we should follow Paul's admonition:

> Whatever you do, do your work heartily, as for the Lord rather than for men; knowing that from the Lord you will receive the reward of the inheritance. It is the Lord Christ whom you serve (Col. 3:23-24).

Those words were not written only to pastors and missionaries. All of us work for Jesus. So we should give Him our very best. When we do, there is a very good chance that we'll succeed in our vocation. And if we succeed, our incomes are more likely to increase. When that happens, it is the time to buck the world's wisdom that says, "Expenses always increase to meet the income." Rather, eternal investments should rise as income increases.

Now let's focus on how you can increase your income for the right reason.

A Plan

Here's a biblical proverb that succinctly reveals the most foundational secret to increasing one's wealth:

> Where no oxen are, the manger [or *stall*] is clean, but much increase comes by the strength of the ox (Prov. 14:4).

A more literal translation of the original Hebrew would read, "No oxen, clean stall; strong bull, much money." Let me shorten that even more: "No manure, no moola."

Who wants to shovel manure to clean out the stall of their ox? Not me! And that is one very good reason not to own an ox. But who wants to plow two acres by hand to prepare his field for planting? Again, not me! So I need to weigh the *burden* of owning an ox against the *blessing* of owning one. And that is a picture of the predicament we often face that ultimately determines our relative wealth. Generally speaking, we can only gain if we are willing to first relinquish something else, namely time, energy and resources.

For example, if you want to enjoy homegrown tomatoes from your backyard, it is going to cost you. You'll have to buy the seeds, plant them, and hammer some tomato stakes into the ground. You'll have put up a fence to keep the varmints out and tie up the tomato plants as they launch skyward. You could, of course, just go a farmer's market or produce store and buy some tomatoes, but they'll expect some of your money, money you had to earn through work.

If you want to earn the salary of a software engineer, you'll have to invest in the necessary education. That will cost money. If you don't have the money, you'll have no choice but to borrow it, spending your hopeful future earnings, which involves risk.

All of this is to say that there is no way to increase your income without investment of time, energy, knowledge and/or resources. Period.

Just about everyone, even the poorest of people, have something they can invest, if nothing more than some time and muscle power. So if you want to increase your income, take an inventory of what you have—no matter how little it is—then invest it so that there is a good chance you'll gain. When you do realize some gain, invest again. Some people who have done that—starting with very little—have become extraordinarily wealthy through continued reinvestment year after year. But they are people who decided to keep shoveling ox manure in its various forms, whether by taking their first job on the graveyard shift, studying hard for their biology exam, or being willing to manage 100 persnickety employees. *Gain always comes from loss, but a loss that is calculated to result in gain.*

I happen to be writing this book on an Apple computer. Three young men, the most famous of whom is the late Steve Jobs, started Apple in 1976. They created and sold a few of their hand-built computer kits called the "Apple I." By borrowing money, using the most current electronic technologies and knowledge, applying hard work and persevering through challenging ups and downs, and by reinvesting gains, Apple has grown to become the world's largest company measured by market capitalization,[1] employing about 50,000 people worldwide. Hundreds of people have become millionaires because of Apple's success. At the time of this writing, Apple has $76 billion on hand in cash and marketable securities. They could have plateaued at any time if they had wanted, but they kept shoveling the manure.

Manure-shoveling maniacs usually end up with just a lot of manure.

Most hard-working people eventually, and rightfully, reach their threshold of tolerance as they weigh the burdens against the blessings that the burdens produce. When the payoff is not worth the manure that must be shoveled, they park, and so they should. How tragic it is when people sacrifice relationships with God and family in order to gain wealth. Balance is the key. Manure-shoveling maniacs usually end up with just a lot of manure.

Again, the key is simply to invest time, resources and money, and then use your gains to invest again so that over time, the gains multiply. Trying to get rich quickly is generally doomed to failure, as it is an attempt to gain a lot by investing only a little. Scripture says, "A man with an evil eye hastens after wealth, and does not know that want will come upon him" (Prov. 28:22). In the Bible, an "evil eye" is a figure of speech for greed. Those

---

[1] As of August 10, 2011, when Apple's market cap was 339 billion dollars.

who, for example, play the lottery—regardless of how poor they are—are greedy, hoping to get rich from their tiny investment. There is a vast difference in moral character between those kinds of folks and the people who gradually increase their wealth over years of hard work and reinvestment of their gains.[2] And among them, those at the pinnacle of wisdom are those who have learned contentment, live far below their means, and have used their gains to lay up treasure in heaven.

From the perspective of eternity, however, the person who wisely builds wealth through work and reinvestment throughout his life yet who fails to lay up treasure in heaven is ultimately just as foolish as the person who buys lottery tickets every week of his life. Neither has any eternal reward.

But what if you make an investment that produces no gain? Actually, such a thing is not possible. Every investment results in gain, if only a gain in wisdom to not make another similar investment. It has been said, "Good judgment is usually the result of experience, and experience frequently the result of bad judgment."

Most successful people have had their share of failures along the way, but they didn't look at their failures as failures, but rather as discoveries of what to avoid in the future. Setbacks can be setups for future gain when wisdom is gained and applied. Thomas Edison declared, "I have not failed. I've just found 10,000 ways that won't work."

Turning Spare Time Into Money

Perhaps the greatest asset that most everyone has that can be used as an investment towards future gain is spare time. We all

---

[2] And, *generally speaking*, that is the fundamental difference between successful and non-successful people. Lazy people, whom the Scriptures denounce, are unwilling to invest the time, work and resources that it takes to be more successful. They chose the clean stall rather than the profit-making strength of an ox. They quickly plateau.

have the choice of wasting our spare time in meaningless activity or investing it by doing something profitable—like gaining knowledge and wisdom. Generally speaking, it is what people know that determines their income. Yes, there are ways of earning an income with a lot of muscle and just a little bit of brain, but even the muscles need the brain to tell them what to do! And the highest-paying jobs among those that require physical labor are those that also require specialized skills or knowledge.

As you gain more specialized knowledge, you join a group of people who are in shorter supply, which means higher demand and higher income. That is why brain surgeons earn more than nurses, and why nurses earn more than Wal-mart greeters. That is also one reason why some realtors make a lot more money than other realtors. Much of it comes down to what they know.

It is for this reason that, within the catalog of wise sayings found in the book of Proverbs, you won't find a single admonition to build bigger muscles. You will, however, find numerous admonitions like the one found in Proverbs 23:23: "Get wisdom and instruction and understanding." And that can be done as easily as surfing the internet, making a trip to your local library and checking out a book for free or, for a reasonable price, by enrolling in a class at your local community college…or by finding a successful mentor.

One area of knowledge that many people lack is that of how to relate to other people. Regardless of what you do, chances are you are going to work with other people. Your success has a lot to do with how well you can get along with them. If you have trouble in that regard, you are less likely to be promoted, and you may find yourself first on the list when layoffs are announced. If you are self-employed or in sales, people skills are generally essential.

So why not invest in what will help you succeed in your relationships? The classic resource to that end is available for free at your local library, and the title is *How to Win Friends and Influence People* by Dale Carnegie. A more contemporary author whom I have grown to appreciate is Dani Johnson, who not only teaches about people skills, but also about many other topics related to financial and family success. Dani is a living testimony to her own teaching, going from being homeless to a multi-millionaire who, along with her husband, Hans, are sowing millions of dollars into worthy ministries (including *Heaven's Family*, by the way). Dani has lots of good information at her website (DaniJohnson. com).

> **When you have the interests of others at heart and help them succeed, you will reap what you sow.**

The essential rule for successful relationships was of course coined by Jesus, who said, "Treat others the same way you want them to treat you" (Luke 6:31). If you do that, you are bound to succeed. When you have the interests of others at heart and help them succeed, you will reap what you sow.

Investing Money

What about investing money? Is that a legitimate way to earn income for the purpose of laying up treasure in heaven? Or is that a form of laying up treasure on earth?

The answer depends on several factors. Let's say you have $100,000 that can be immediately invested in heaven or invested on earth in hopes of generating a return that will be invested in heaven. You'd need to generate about a 7 percent annual return on your investment for ten years before it would double in value and thus enable you to give away $100,000 and still have the original investment, which then could be used to continue to generate income to lay up in heaven. Of course, if inflation is taken into consideration, you would need to generate considerably more than a 7 percent annual return in order to actually double the purchasing power of your $100,000 in ten years. Still, eventually, a consistently profitable investment has the real potential to enable an investor/giver to lay up more treasure in heaven than he would have had he given away his potential investment at the start. His investment can be a blessing even after he dies. (Although I am not sure the Lord would credit him at that point, since we are promised rewards for "deeds in the body"; see 2 Cor 5:10.)

Of course, you wouldn't have to wait ten years to start giving away earnings on an investment. If you realized a 7 percent increase the first year on your $100,000, you could give away $7,000 and still have your original $100,000. In such a case, however, because you would lose the benefit of compounding interest, it would take you a little over 14 years at 7 percent before you could give away $100,000 total, the same amount you could have immediately given away had you not invested your $100,000.

Then there is the very real risk that your investment will not increase in value, but decrease, and you'll have even less to lay up in heaven. On the other hand, your investment might increase more than 7 percent per year, enabling you to more quickly reach the time when your investment can result in more treasure in heaven than it would have had you not invested it.

All of this is to say, there is no pat answer. The safest action to take is to not invest on earth, but rather lay up your potential investment in heaven immediately where it can't be lost. If however, you are knowledgeable about investing and have a long-range plan, the safest plan may not be the best plan. So you need to pray to seek the Lord's wisdom. And it goes without saying that we should never invest in any business or company that makes a profit doing things that God hates. In such a case, we would be partners in their sin. For that reason, beware of mutual funds, as fund managers may invest your God-given money in what God hates.

Lending at Interest

Some Christians are persuaded that investing money in hopes of gain and lending money at interest (including earning interest on bank deposits) are fundamentally wrong because the latter is prohibited in the Old Testament. For example, God declared in the Law of Moses:

> If you lend money to My people, to the poor among you, you are not to act as a creditor to him; you shall not charge him interest. If you ever take your neighbor's cloak as a pledge, you are to return it to him before the sun sets, for that is his only covering; it is his cloak for his body. What else shall he sleep in? And it shall come about that when he cries out to Me, I will hear him, for I am gracious (Ex. 22:25-27).

Notice, however, that God was specifically speaking of profiting by loaning to the poor (see also Lev. 22:35-38). In fact, He was speaking of lending to people who are so poor that the only collateral they could offer was their outer coat. It is easy to understand why God would forbid lending at interest to people in such dire circumstances, people who were borrowing for mere survival.

But was God forbidding lending at interest to others, besides the desperately poor?

No. In fact, God also declared in the Mosaic Law: "You may charge interest to a foreigner" (Deut. 23:20). So obviously some lending at interest was acceptable.

Certainly there is nothing wrong with lending money at interest to people who intend to use their loans to make money through business or investment. It is only right that, if the borrower prospers from his loan, he should share some of his profits with the lender who was partly responsible, through his sacrifice, for the borrower's success.

In our day, when currencies are not backed by anything tangible or valuable such as gold, and when governments keep printing more currency and fueling inflation, the person who loans at no interest becomes a giver as well as a loaner, as he accepts less repayment than what he loaned due to the erosion of the currency's value. Most people don't realize that the U.S. dollar (as of 2012) has lost 96 percent of its purchasing power since 1913. What cost $20 in the year I was born (1958) now costs $156. That's an inflation rate of 681 percent.[3]

The Lesson:

We only have one opportunity to lay up treasure in heaven—while we are on the earth. This is the classic "once-in-a-lifetime opportunity," and it ought to motive us make all the money we can so that we can lay up as much treasure in heaven as possible.

All earthly financial gain is a result of investment of time, talents and treasures. (No manure, no moola.) The same is true of heavenly gain since it originates as earthy gain. (No manure, no transferable moola.) Shovel hard and shovel smart!

---

[3] See www.coinnews.net/tools/cpi-inflation-calculator/ to calculate the rate of U.S. inflation for any time span since 1913.

CHAPTER SIX

Discriminating Deposits

We've covered a lot of ground so far, and I'm glad you're still with me. That's a good sign. You know that your life is a journey to stand before Jesus, the Venture Capitalist before whom you will have to give an account of your time, talents and treasures. You understand that you are among the world's wealthy elite, and "to whom much is given, much is required." You are taking action to eliminate foolish debt, to self-dispossess, and to scale down in Disneyland so you can lay up treasure in heaven. You are an intelligent investor, leveraging your time and resources for maximum earthly gain. And you have long-range investment plans for the remainder of your life and on into eternity. Feel good! You are on the right track!

In this chapter, we're going to think about the mechanics of laying up treasure in heaven. I'm going to say some things that could be considered controversial, particularly to those who, for selfish reasons, prefer that the truth remains hidden. But I'll back up my claims with Scripture, and I dare anyone to prove that my conclusions are wrong. Are you ready? Good!

The Means to Laying Up Heavenly Treasures

Jesus clearly taught that the way to lay up treasure in heaven is by giving to charity on earth:

> Sell your possessions and give to charity; make your-selves money belts which do not wear out, an unfailing

treasure in heaven, where no thief comes near nor moth destroys (Luke 12:33).

The version of the Bible from which I have just quoted is the *New American Standard Version*. Among Bible translations, it essentially stands alone with the translation, "give to charity." All others say something like, "give to the poor," "give to the needy, " or "give alms." Of course, to "give alms" is to give to the poor. All of this is to say that when Jesus told His followers how to lay up treasures in heaven, He specifically instructed them to give to the poor, and not just to "charities" in general.

I think you can understand why your gifts to some charities would not result in treasure being laid up in heaven for your benefit. For example, it would seem very doubtful that gifts to the Community Opera Association, Ducks Unlimited, or National Public Radio would be credited to your heavenly bank account. Those causes don't benefit the poor. Rather, they essentially provide services for the people who support them. People usually give to those kinds of organizations because they appreciate what those kinds of organizations do that benefits them.

So it is important that we think about whom we give to or what charities we contribute to if we hope to lay up treasure in heaven through our giving. You can't just give to anyone or anything and expect a heavenly return. If, for example, you deposit money into your local library's book return thinking that you are making a deposit in your bank's ATM machine, you are going to be disappointed when you return to the library to inquire about your account balance!

It is significant that every time Scripture records Jesus speaking about the means to laying up treasures in heaven, giving to the poor is the means. We've already read Jesus' words in that regard to His disciples found in Luke 12:33 (see above). The three other scriptural records that reveal the means to laying up treasures in heaven are Matthew, Mark and Luke's reporting of Jesus' conversation with the rich young ruler. In each of those three accounts, Jesus instructed him to sell his possessions and give the proceeds to the poor. If he would do so, he would have treasure in heaven (see Matt. 19:21, Mark 10:21, Luke 18:22).

All of this is to say that, if we are going to rely on nothing other than what Jesus said (which would hardly seem to be foolish), then the means to laying up treasure in heaven is by giving to the poor.

I did not say, of course, that there are no other worthy causes that deserve our contributions, and I did not say that giving to other worthy causes never results in treasures being laid up in heaven. I did say, however, that if we are going to rely only on what Jesus said, then giving to the poor is the means to laying up treasures in heaven.

> **The means to laying up treasure in heaven is by giving to the poor.**

And certainly, when we consider all that the New Testament has to say about giving, giving to the poor stands out as preeminent. For these reasons, we certainly ought to take a look at where we're giving. If little or none of our giving is directed to the poor, then we need to make an adjustment.

An Important Question

Sadly, so many Christians have been conditioned to give only to the churches that they attend and, worse, little or none of what they give to their churches finds its way to the poor.

It would be good to ask ourselves, "How are my contributions to my church different than the contributions that people make to the Community Opera Association, Ducks Unlimited, or National Public Radio?" As I've already said, people give to those organizations to perpetuate the benefits that they enjoy from those organizations. Their giving is selfishly motivated. Similarly, people generally give to their churches to help perpetuate the benefits that they enjoy from their churches. Their contributions pay for their pastors' salaries, the mortgage, utilities and so on, so that ministry to their families, and church fellowship with others, can continue.

Praise God for any percentage of their contributions that is passed on from the church to the poor, but even then, the "poor" are often church members facing tough times yet who are still quite wealthy in comparison to the world's truly poor. They often don't fit the description of the "least of these."

Now don't become angry with me! Love me, because I'm telling you truth that could make a positive difference in your eternal future. Can you imagine standing before Jesus after faithfully tithing to your local church for decades, and hearing Him say, "You laid up no treasure in heaven. You basically tithed to yourself all those years"?

Here is an undeniable New Testament fact: There is not a single example in the New Testament of any believer giving money for anything related to a church building (such as a building program, mortgage, Sunday School annex, new carpeting, utilities and so on), nor is there a record of any believer being encouraged to give to anything related to a church building. The simple reason is because the early believers—for the first three hundred years after Jesus walked the earth—predominantly met in homes (see Rom 16:5, 1 Cor. 16:19, Col. 4:15, Philem 2).[1]

For the Record...

When we read about giving in the New Testament, it was always the type of giving that assisted the needy or sustained

---

[1] Think of how much good could have been done if the money that has been spent on church buildings over the past 1,700 years had been used for the sake of the poor and for the spread of the gospel!

needy vocational ministers. That is it!

Consider the record found in the Book of Acts. The very first mention of giving by the early Christians is found in the second chapter:

> And all those who had believed were together, and had all things in common; and they began selling their property and possessions, and were sharing them with all, as anyone might have need (Acts 2:44-45).

First, note their common self-dispossession. The apostles were doing just what Jesus told them to do—they were teaching their disciples to obey everything that Jesus had commanded them (see Matt. 28:19-20). So they taught their disciples to self-dispossess as Jesus had taught them, and the early Christians wisely began transferring their wealth where it could never be lost.

Second, note that the giving of the early believers was directed towards the needy.

The second description of giving by the early Christians is similar to the first:

> And the congregation of those who believed were of one heart and soul; and not one of them claimed that anything belonging to him was his own; but all things were common property to them. And with great power the apostles were giving witness to the resurrection of the Lord Jesus, and abundant grace was upon them all. For there was not a needy person among them, for all who were owners of land or houses would sell them and bring the proceeds of the sales, and lay them at the apostles' feet; and they would be distributed to each, as any had need (Acts 4:32-34).

Again, note the common self-dispossession. And note that the beneficiaries of their obedience to Christ were the needy.

Incidentally, I don't think we should conclude that those believers who owned only one house sold their house to lay the proceeds at the apostles' feet. It would seem more likely that those who owned "houses," that is, more than one, sold their extra homes. (See Acts 2:46; 5:42; 8:3; 12:12; 20:20; 21:8 for indications that early Christians continued to own houses). A home provides the necessity of shelter, a place to share meals, enjoy church gatherings and welcome strangers (see Matt. 25:43).

Additional Evidence

In Acts 6:1-6, we learn that the early Christians cared for widows by means of a daily serving of food. The apostles themselves initially administrated that daily serving, underscoring its importance to them. I think it is safe to assume that the food that was served to the widows was purchased using money that was given by the early Christians. So we have yet another example of giving that is directed to the poor.

In Acts 9:36-39, we learn of a devoted disciple named Tabitha who was "abounding in deeds of kindness and charity, which she continually did" (Acts 9:36). Specifically, we learn that she made clothing for poor widows (see Acts 9:39). Jesus eventually would say to her, "I was naked, and you clothed Me" (Matt. 25:35-36).

In Acts 11:27-30, we read that any of the disciples in Antioch who had means contributed to an offering to assist poor believers in Judea.

We search in vain in the book of Acts for even a hint that any of the giving of early Christians was directed toward purchasing, constructing or maintaining buildings. *All giving was directed to the poor.*

And when we look for some indication in Acts that any giving was directed towards vocational ministers, we can't find anything (although we know from reading Paul's letters that he was often supported through the gifts of believers). In Acts 18:1-5, however, we read of Paul supporting himself through tent making. And when he once gathered the elders/pastors/overseers (synonymous words) from Ephesus, he reminded them:

> I have coveted no one's silver or gold or clothes. You yourselves know that these hands ministered to my own needs and to the men who were with me. In everything I showed you that by working hard in this manner you must help the weak and remember the words of the Lord Jesus, that He Himself said, "It is more blessed to give than to receive" (Acts 20:33-35).

Obviously, discipling a small group of people who gather in a house, as did the Ephesian elders/pastors/overseers, would not require one's full time. Thus, the elders/pastors/overseers to whom Paul was speaking could follow his good example of working hard in some vocation to support themselves. What a far cry are Paul's words to those men in comparison to modern prosperity preachers who tell their followers, "If you want God's blessing, you need to bless the man of God!" May God have mercy on their souls.

Needy Ministers

If I wanted to make this a longer book, we could look at giving as it is portrayed in the four Gospels and the epistles. That study would underscore the fact that the large majority of giving under the ministry of Christ and in the early church was directed to the poor. Even in those cases where we find some mention of people giving to support Jesus and His band or the apostles after Jesus' ascension, those would also be cases of giving to the needy, as there were no wealthy ministers (like there are today).

Paul's words in 1 Corinthians 4:11 come to mind: "To this present hour we are both hungry and thirsty, and are poorly clothed, and are roughly treated, and are homeless."

So is caring for the poor as important to modern Christians as it was to early Christians? It would seem not. And when multitudes of pastors have never so much as given a single sermon on the topic, and they teach their congregations that "the tithe belongs to the local church," and those tithes end up being spent on serving the people who gave them, is it any wonder that caring for the poor is a non-existent element of the spiritual lives of many professing Christians?

> Is caring for the poor as important to modern Christians as it was to early Christians?

This is even more astounding in light of all that Jesus taught about caring for the poor, even going so far as to reveal that the authenticity of one's profession of faith, as well as one's eternal destiny, is determined by whether or not one met the pressing needs of those in His family who lacked food, water, clothing, shelter and health (see Matt. 25:31-46). If we believe what Jesus said, there are, tragically, many goats among the sheep today.

Hopefully you are persuaded that your giving should be directed towards the poor if you want to lay up treasures in heaven. Is there anything else you should know? Yes. I can think of three very important things, two of which I'll share in this chapter. I'll cover the third in the next chapter.

Numbers One and Two

First, Scripture teaches that our first responsibility is to help fellow believers. Paul wrote, "So then, while we have opportunity, let us do good to all men, and *especially to those who are of the household of the faith*" (Gal. 6:10, emphasis added). The "least of these"—of whom Jesus spoke in His foretelling of the judgment of the sheep and the goats—are not just any poor people. They are members of His spiritual family, His "brothers" (Matt. 25:40) as He said. Those are the ones whom we want to assist first.

Second, recognize that what is called "poverty" in developed nations is not poverty. You'd be hard pressed to find very many of the "least of these" in the Western world—believers who lack food, water, clothing or shelter, or who can't get access to those things with a little effort. (Although you could certainly find plenty who are sick or in prison who could be visited, and such persons are also listed as being among the "least of these" by Jesus in Matthew 25:31-46.)

In the United States, the average household defined as "poor" by the federal government enjoys a car, refrigerator, stove, clothes washer and dryer, microwave, two color televisions, a DVD player, and they live in a house or apartment equipped with cable or satellite TV and air conditioning. The average *poor* American has more living space than the average European. In 2011, the federal government set the poverty line for a family of four at an annual income of $22,350.

In contrast, half of the world's population lives on less than $2.50 per day, less than $1,000 per year. So, for simplicity's sake, we can say that at least half of the members of Christ's body live on less than $2.50 per day. Obviously helping believers caught in that kind of poverty should have priority over helping believers who are having trouble making their monthly $1,200 mortgage payment.

How to Help

Chances are, you don't have contact with impoverished Christians living on less than $2.50 per day. So how can you serve them? There are several options.

Perhaps you have received communication from poor people overseas (who somehow obtained your email address) and who are asking for your help. I *strongly* recommend that you proceed with *great* caution, because there are multitudes of unscrupulous people in developing nations who prey on compassionate Christians through email appeals. They can quote the Bible, send you photos of the children in their orphanages, write heart-touching prayers, send scans of their ministerial credentials and letters of recommendation from other ministers, invite you to visit them, and make you feel terribly guilty, but they are wolves in sheep's clothing.

If you fly to their country to actually visit their ministry and see their living conditions, they will be waiting to deceive you even more. I've once visited an "orphanage" of forty children in Pakistan that I later learned was nothing more than a temporary gathering of neighborhood kids. It was run by a Jesus-loving, Bible-quoting "businessman," whose business was to defraud as many Western Christians as he could. He is still in that business today. And the world is full of such people.

A better option is finding a Western missionary who lives in a poor nation who could serve as your bridge to very poor believers. Missionaries are "on the ground," working full-time in one location, so they have a better chance of discerning the real needs of genuine saints from the contrived needs of crooks. (If you do select this option, I suggest designating at least 10 percent of your gift to the missionary who administers your gift. Missionaries, like everyone else, can't work for free.)

At the ministry that I direct, *Heaven's Family*, we prefer to partner with Western missionaries, rather than indigenous ministers, in order to serve the "least of these," because they are less likely to embezzle ministry funds. Entrusting an indigenous person who lives on $5 a day with $2,000 is like entrusting a Westerner with $50,000 or $100,000. Thus the temptation to pilfer from that $2,000 is greater for the indigenous minister than for the average Western missionary.[2]

A third option is to employ the services of a trustworthy ministry organization that serves the poor. There are many such organizations, but I can speak best about the one that I direct, *Heaven's Family*. We're currently serving the "least of these" in more than 30 nations with the help of about 120 expatriate and indigenous partners.

Our Core Principles

When we started *Heaven's Family*, we were determined to never exploit the poor, making money for ourselves through their plight. So we've created about 25 focused funds that each serve a certain category of people—such as orphans, widows, the persecuted, the ill, the hungry, and so on. When compassionate donors contribute to any of those funds, 100 percent of what they give is sent overseas to help those who meet each fund's criteria. Nothing is taken for administration, as all our administrative costs are paid from our general fund (to which donors can also choose to contribute). In this way, we are able to purely serve the poor without personal gain.

We also do our best to keep our administrative costs as low as possible. Many of our employees raise all or part of their personal support, or they have side businesses, so they effectively work for *Heaven's Family* for free or for much less than they are worth. They are a very special group of people. And no one is being paid a high salary. I've never understood the justification of those organizations that ask you to donate so they can feed starving children, but whose president keeps $500,000 of what donors send to feed those starving children for his or her salary.

---

[2] This is not to say, however, that indigenous ministers can never be trusted, or that all Western missionaries can be trusted. The important thing is to know with whom you are working. Trust is something that must be earned.

No one at *Heaven's Family* makes more than the average salary of comparable employees at similar-sized nonprofit organizations. As the president, I make less than half of what the average CEO makes at similar-sized nonprofit organizations.[3]

Trustworthy organizations have nothing to hide, thus they do their best to be financially transparent. All nonprofits in the U.S. are required to submit a detailed annual financial report to the Internal Revenue Service by means of Form 990. All 990 Forms are required by law to be available for public inspection. (*Heaven's Family* keeps our most recent 990 Form posted on our website.)

By looking at an organization's 990 Form, you can find out the salaries of its highest-paid employees, plus what percentage of its contributions are used for programs, fund-raising, and administration. The best nonprofits usually spend 10 to 20 percent of their income for fund raising and administration. I would beware of any organization that claims less than 10 percent for those items, as I would suspect that they aren't telling the truth, or they are entrusting large sums of money to indigenous partners with insufficient accountability from them. Serving the poor with excellence in developing countries requires lots of administration.

The third important principle you need to know in order to effectively lift the poor from poverty is so important that I've reserved the entire next chapter for it. I suspect you will be surprised by what you read—and enlightened.

---

[3] These figures are based on a detailed survey of over 900 nonprofit organizations.

CHAPTER SEVEN

When Free Becomes Expensive

Giving money to the poor has the potential of keeping them poor. Not understanding that, many well-meaning Christians have inadvertently hurt those whom they've wanted to help. I first began to understand this back in the late 1980s, when I had an opportunity to travel inside the Eastern European nation of Romania, taking a trip that gave me an education on the economic "advantages" of communism.

Romania was then suffering under its fifth decade of communism. It was a nation that was crumbling. I saw empty store shelves, food lines, and the dreary faces of people in survival mode.

One of the few happy people whom I met in Romania was an elderly pastor who lived in a weathered little wooden house in a rural village. He was, in fact, bubbling with joy, and he told me that the reason he was so blessed was because he loved God with all his heart, mind, soul and strength. Visiting with him was a delight.

Pastors were considered societal parasites in Eastern Europe during those years, and so he, like all pastors, was required to work at a daily job that was thought by communist leaders to be of some economic value. He had been assigned to work with a crew of loggers. He told me that each day his crew would hike out into the forest, cut down trees for three hours, and then lie down and sleep on the forest floor for the remainder of their shift.

I asked him the reason for such an extended daily work break. He explained that if his crew cut down more than their required quota of trees on any given day, their daily quota would be increased. And they would not receive any increase in pay since the government set all wages, and everyone in Romania was supposedly equal. So that joyful, blessed pastor who loved God with all his heart spent his afternoons sleeping in the woods!

His story illustrates a universal human trait: Unless we are motivated by some noble cause, we will always choose the easiest option. That Romanian pastor did not consider lining the pockets of communist bureaucrats to be a noble cause. If he, however, would have had a guarantee of earning more money in exchange for more work, he would have worked harder, as he would have been motivated by love for his wife and children to be a better provider. He may have also been motivated by love for the poor with whom he could share a portion of his earnings.

Communism utterly kills people's motivation to work harder, because the harder-working laborer receives no benefit. Socialism has the same effect, just to a lesser degree. Why should I work harder if most of my increase is taken by the government and given to someone else who is unwilling to work?

Putting Yourself in His Romanian Shoes

What would you have done had you been that Romanian pastor? If you don't know, I can help you.

Imagine for a moment that you were looking for a job and were offered two identical opportunities, but one job paid more than the other. Which would you choose? You would, of course, choose the higher-paying opportunity simply because it offers you more money for the same amount of work.

Now back to that Romanian pastor. He was similarly motivated, except there was a ceiling set on his earnings. So he chose the "higher paying job"—the one that required less work for the same amount of earnings. If you or I had been that Romanian pastor, we would have been sleeping in the woods every afternoon, too.

Let me take this one step further. What if you were offered two opportunities to gain $1,000, one that required one week's labor, and one that required no labor? I suspect you'd take the second offer, the gift of $1,000. Again, unless we're motivated by some noble cause, we naturally choose the easiest option.

Understanding this helps us realize what we don't want to do for the poor if we truly want to help them, and that is, continually give them something for nothing. *A flow of well-intentioned charity can ensure perpetual poverty.* We should not wonder why the poor have no motivation to work when we feed, clothe and house them without requiring any work from them. Like the former communist government of Romania, we effectively kill any motivation they may have had before we arrived with all our good intentions.

Government charity is of course no different than private charity. If by working people are not able to earn significantly more money than they can gain from collecting welfare checks, they will have absolutely no motivation to get "off the dole" (as they say in Britain).

Help that Hurts

When it comes to dealing with the truly poor in less-developed nations—those whose poverty is appalling by comparison to what is labeled as poverty in the more-developed world—we have a natural tendency to compassionately empty our wallets to instantly meet their glaring needs. But the beneficiary has been taught a lesson that he will not soon forget: The easiest means to money is to be friends with rich people from other countries. That is the breeding ground for all sorts of evil that aid organizations and compassionate people frequently find themselves facing, evils such as deception, flattery, and bad reports about other "less-worthy" beneficiaries.

Beyond that, expectations and dependencies are slowly created, and as benefactors slowly grow weary of feeding the ever-increasing appetites of the monsters they've created, they ultimately stop their flow of charity. In the bitter end, benefactors find themselves accused of 'betrayal" and "cold-heartedness" by their former beneficiaries—who have already begun to search for their next benefactor.

Before I continue, let me quickly affirm that needy people who are unable to earn a living for themselves, such as orphaned children, elderly widows, those who are significantly handicapped or oppressed, and those with no earning opportunities, are in a different category.

Development is better than relief.

They need a flow of charity, at least temporarily. Similarly, those who suddenly find themselves in desperate situations, such as victims of natural disasters or war refugees, need immediate handouts in the form of food and shelter. Yet even in those cases, relief needs to transition to development as soon as possible. And although I hoped to avoid using the worn-out cliché about the comparative benefits of giving a man a fish versus teaching him to fish, there is no better illustration of what I'm talking about. Development is better than relief.

It is not always quite so simple in the real world, however, because chances are the man already knows how to fish, and he is already fishing, but he is only catching enough fish to barely feed himself and his family. What he needs is a boat and a net so he can catch more fish, and he needs a nearby market where people would be willing to buy his fish.

So how do we get that man the boat and net he needs? We have two good options. We can either give or lend him money to purchase the tools a fisherman needs. If we *give* him money, from the outset the profits from his new venture don't have to be split between meeting his own needs and making loan payments. He may not, however, be as careful to take care of the tools that cost him nothing, and he may not work as hard to ensure his success. What costs nothing is often valued accordingly. If he fails, he hasn't lost anything, and is only back to where he was before he started. He may assume that if he fails, his benefactor will be there to bail him out again.

If, however, we lend him money at interest to purchase a boat and net—and even require some collateral—he is then motivated to carefully consider his business plan, weigh his risk of loss, and work very hard to succeed. He is personally invested from the start. Moreover, if he repays his loan, we can then help another needy fisherman to buy a boat and net, and then another, and another and another. If he refuses to take a loan (at a reasonable interest rate), it might be a good indication that he doesn't believe he can succeed in the proposed business. The willingness of people to take loans and put up collateral can be an excellent litmus test of their chances of success.

Learning these things from our experiences and the experiences of others, *Heaven's Family* is focusing more and more on establishing micro-banks. These banks not only provide start-up capital via loans for enterprising believers, but they also provide income for micro-bankers via the interest that their little banks earn.

Liberating the Lazy

If we truly want to help the poor, we should never do for the poor what they can do for themselves. Years ago I can remember traveling with my church's youth group to Appalachia to repair run-down houses of the poorest people I had ever met up until that point in my life. The people spoke English, but we were barely able to understand them because of their thick mountain accents. And I remember how we marveled that the residents would just sit and watch us repair their leaky roofs and sagging porches. We never required them to join us in our work, and they were happy to drink our lemonade and not get in our way.

If I had to do it all over again, I would start by asking homeowners if they had any roof leaks. If they said "yes," I'd offer them a few shingles, some roofing nails and a can of tar if they would promise to go to work immediately on fixing their leaks while I watched.

> ## "If anyone is not willing to work, then he is not to eat, either" (2 Thes. 3:10)

Scripture says, "If anyone is not willing to work, then he is not to eat, either" (2 Thes. 3:10). That is plain and simple, and it is just as much a biblical commandment as are all the commandments to give to the poor. The apostle Paul believed in that commandment so much that he worked just to set a good example, even when he had the right to be sustained by the offerings:

> For you yourselves know how you ought to follow our example, because we did not act in an undisciplined manner among you, nor did we eat anyone's bread without paying for it, but with labor and hardship we kept working night and day so that we would not be a burden to any of you; not because we do not have the right to this, but in order to offer ourselves as a model for you, so that you would follow our example. For even when we were with you, we used to give you this order: if anyone is not willing to work, then he is not to eat, either (2 Thes. 3:7-10).

Under the old covenant, field owners were forbidden to gather the gleanings from their fields during the harvest, but to leave what remained for the poor (see Deut. 24:19-21; Lev. 19:9-10). Take note, however, that if the poor were to benefit, they had to work to gather the gleanings. Field owners didn't deliver gleanings to their doorsteps.

God set a personal example in that regard, freely pouring manna from heaven six days a week for the needy people of Israel as they journeyed to the Promised Land. He required, however, that they gather it. Those who didn't work didn't eat. There was no such thing as a free lunch from God.

We read in Acts 6 of the early church's efforts to take care of widows by means of a daily feeding. It didn't take long before the apostles were plagued by the universal dilemma that always stalks the generous: More needy people started showing up for their handouts. Those widows in Jerusalem who were being overlooked started complaining, and their representatives accused the apostles of ethnic favoritism. That is no doubt why the apostles, as they decided to delegate their responsibilities to others, required men who were "full of the Spirit and of wisdom" (Acts 6:3). Effective benevolence demands great wisdom, lest more harm than good be done.

Paul later wisely laid out very detailed instructions to Timothy regarding which widows should and should not be supported by the church (see 1 Tim. 5:3-16). Only a limited number would qualify, and those who did would hardly be receiving something for nothing, as they were required to work full-time in serving others, doing good works, and praying.

I've found that in some cases, impoverished Christians in other countries have been so conditioned by the thoughtless charity of Western Christians that they seem to have no concept of working to earn money, but expect to be sustained by never-ending handouts. If offered a loan to start a business, they refuse it, as it requires work to succeed and repay the loan. Those folks should be left alone until their stomachs educate their heads, as Proverbs tells us: "A worker's appetite works for him, for his hunger urges him on" (Prov. 16:26).

Flushing Out the Sluggards

I once heard about a pastor who, during the Great Depression, frequently had beggars come to his church office to ask him for money. He would first ask them if they had looked for a job. They would respond that they had, but explained that they had simply not been able to find work. He then asked them if they would work if they could find a job. They always replied in the affirmative. Finally, he would say to them, "Good! I have a pile of wood in back of the church that needs to be split. There's an axe beside the woodshed. Go out and split as many of those logs as you can, and then come back and I'll fairly pay you."

The majority of the time, those freeloaders politely thanked him, walked out his door, and he never saw them again. And that pastor kept a clear conscience in the process.

God wants us to help the poor, but the best way to help them is to help them lift themselves out of poverty. He doesn't want us to help sluggards remain lazy.

Go to the ant, O sluggard, observe her ways and be wise, which, having no chief, officer or ruler, prepares her food in the summer and gathers her provision in the harvest. How long will you lie down, O sluggard? When will you arise from your sleep? "A little sleep, a little slumber, a little folding of the hands to rest"—Your poverty will come in like a vagabond and your need like an armed man (Prov. 6:6-11).

CHAPTER EIGHT

The Eternal Upgrade

This is the final chapter, so let's think about the day when we'll begin to benefit from our investments in heaven. That will be payday—a day when we surely won't regret any earthly sacrifice that we made. In fact, we're likely to regret that we didn't make greater earthly sacrifices. On that day we will see the treasure we've laid up in heaven.

So when we arrive, will we be able to log on to our accounts at HeavenBank.com to check our current balances—balances that will be based on our earthly financial sacrifices? Will we be able to make withdrawals to purchase mansions at the corners of Diamond Road and Emerald Avenue, complete with three-chariot garages?

Those are interesting questions, and I wish I knew the answers. We do know that life in heaven (and ultimately on the new earth) will be similar in many ways to life as we know it now. Heaven will be populated with multitudes of people (Rev. 7:9). They will all have places to reside (see John 14:2-3). They'll be able to walk and talk and enjoy heaven's beauty. It will be a place full of activity. The Bible certainly doesn't portray heaven as a place where people just sit around all day on clouds strumming golden harps.

Will there be learning? Creativity? I can't imagine not. Work? Progress? How about ownership, labor and commerce? If so, will everyone work purely from joy, and will there be no incentive to gain something through our labors? Will there be some medium of exchange? I wish I knew the answers to all those questions.

Regardless, we know that Jesus told us that we can and should lay up treasure in heaven. That implies that those who do will have something waiting for them in heaven that they would not have had otherwise. What will it be? Does every dollar given away on earth add a gold coin to our safe deposit box at Heaven Bank?

I can't resist mentioning a story that is told of a man whom Saint Peter saw dragging two large suitcases with him as he trudged toward the pearly gates. Upon his arrival, he breathlessly dropped the suitcases with a thud. Peter asks, "What's in the suitcases?" The man replies, "Let me show you!" He opens them up to reveal to Peter that both are filled with gold coins and bars. Peter responds, "Pavement? You brought pieces of pavement?"

> **When someone loves you so much that He dies for you, you can trust that any rewards He promises are going to be good.**

Of course, just because there are roads in the New Jerusalem that John described as being "pure gold, like transparent glass" (Rev. 21:21) doesn't completely rule out the possibility of gold coins being used in heaven as a medium of exchange. There will be no thieves living in the New Jerusalem, and so no one who lives there will yield to the temptation to sneak out late at night to dig up some of the road (not to mention the fact that there will be no night there).

But back to my primary question: What exactly are the "treasures" that we lay up in heaven? What are the rewards for our obedient stewardship?

Unfortunately, the Bible doesn't reveal as much as I wish it did, and perhaps because our rewards are beyond our current comprehension. Because of that, we're just going to have to trust Jesus on this, which isn't so bad. When someone loves you so much that He dies for you, you can trust that any rewards He promises are going to be good.

Of course, the Bible does speak of crowns that may be received, such as the "crown of righteousness" (2 Tim. 4:8). Everyone who "loved His appearing" (2 Tim. 4:8) will receive that crown, however, and I think it is safe to say that all true followers of Christ "loved His appearing." Similarly, the "crown of life" will be given to all who persevere and love Jesus (see Jas. 1:12, Rev. 2:10). So neither of those two crowns seems to be reserved as special rewards. An "unfading crown of glory" is another one that is mentioned in the New Testament, and it apparently will be granted exclusively to good shepherds (1 Pet. 5:1-4).

We can certainly anticipate receiving praise from God for our sacrifices (see 1 Cor. 4:5). Hearing the words, "Well done, good and faithful slave" (Matt. 25:21) will be a reward that will warm our hearts forever.

Scripture also seems to imply that God will reward us by granting us different positions of authority in Christ's government. Jesus' Parables of the Talents and of the Nobleman support this possibility (see Matt. 25:14-30; Luke 19:12-27). In the Parable of the Nobleman, the two faithful servants are awarded authority over cities. And Scripture teaches that we will rule and reign with Christ in His kingdom (see 2 Tim. 2:12; Rev. 2:26-27, 5:10, 20:6).

Even now, some future seats of authority in God's kingdom are already reserved. Jesus said to the Twelve:

> Truly I say to you, that you who have followed Me, in the regeneration when the Son of Man will sit on His glorious

throne, you also shall sit upon twelve thrones, judging the
twelve tribes of Israel. And everyone who has left houses or
brothers or sisters or father or mother or children or farms
for My name's sake, *shall receive many times as much*, and
shall inherit eternal life (Matt. 19:28-29, emphasis added).

Isn't it true that one consuming desire shared by all of Jesus'
genuine disciples is to be entrusted with more responsibility for
His glory? Do not we all currently wish that our ministries were
more fruitful? Perhaps the greater opportunities that we will be
given to serve Him in His kingdom will fulfill those desires.

Apart from crowns, words of praise, and governmental positions, I suspect that there are still going to be some surprises for
those who have laid up treasure in heaven. 1 Corinthians 2:9
comes to mind: "Things which eye has not seen and ear has not
heard, and which have not entered the heart of man, all that God
has prepared for those who love Him."

When the Last Shall be First

Some have concluded—based upon their interpretation of
Jesus' Parable of the Laborers—that all of the redeemed will receive identical rewards in heaven. But we must not emphasize
one scripture passage at the neglect of all the others. Because
the Bible has only one Author, every verse must be harmonized
with the other 31,000 verses. Let's read the Parable of the Laborers closely:

For the kingdom of heaven is like a landowner who went
out early in the morning to hire laborers for his vineyard.
And when he had agreed with the laborers for a denarius
for the day, he sent them into his vineyard. And he went
out about the third hour and saw others standing idle in
the market place; and to those he said, "You too go into

the vineyard, and whatever is right I will give you." And so they went. Again he went out about the sixth and the ninth hour, and did the same thing. And about the eleventh hour he went out, and found others standing; and he said to them, "Why have you been standing here idle all day long?" They said to him, "Because no one hired us." He said to them, "You too go into the vineyard."

And when evening had come, the owner of the vineyard said to his foreman, "Call the laborers and pay them their wages, beginning with the last group to the first." And when those hired about the eleventh hour came, each one received a denarius. And when those hired first came, they thought that they would receive more; and they also received each one a denarius. And when they received it, they grumbled at the landowner, saying, "These last men have worked only one hour, and you have made them equal to us who have borne the burden and the scorching heat of the day." But he answered and said to one of them, "Friend, I am doing you no wrong; did you not agree with me for a denarius? Take what is yours and go your way, but I wish to give to this last man the same as to you. Is it not lawful for me to do what I wish with what is my own? Or is your eye envious because I am generous?" Thus the last shall be first, and the first last" (Matt. 20:1-16).

Was Jesus trying to teach us that, in the end, everyone will receive the same reward regardless of their labor or faithfulness? I do not believe so. Take note that, as the landowner rewarded each group of laborers, he took into consideration the *opportunities* that they were given to work. The one-hour laborers would gladly have worked a full day *had they been given the opportunity*. But they only had the opportunity to work one hour.

This teaches us that when God rewards us for our service, He will take into consideration the opportunities (and resources) that He entrusted to us. "From everyone who has been given much, much will be required" (Luke 12:48). You can receive as much reward as the world's greatest evangelist if you are just as faithful with the gifts and opportunities that God has granted to you. This principle was clearly illustrated in Scripture's story of the widow who contributed just two small coins to the temple treasury:

> And He sat down opposite the treasury, and began observing how the people were putting money into the treasury; and many rich people were putting in large sums. A poor widow came and put in two small copper coins, which amount to a cent. Calling His disciples to Him, He said to them, "Truly I say to you, this poor widow put in more than all the contributors to the treasury; for they all put in out of their surplus, but she, out of her poverty, put in all she owned, all she had to live on" (Mark 12:41-44).

From God's viewpoint, her tiny contribution was larger than those of the rich because He took into consideration her available resources. She gave all she had to live on. And for that reason, her heavenly reward for her small contribution would surpass the rewards the rich would receive for their large contributions. That is one reason why, at the judgment, "Many who are first will be last, and the last, first" (Mark 10:31).

Incidentally, don't make the mistake of thinking that there is anything selfish about striving to be among those who are first. It is not as if there are a limited number of rewards for which we're all competing. Our limitless God has unlimited rewards. It isn't selfish to strive to be among the first because you don't have to push anyone down to make it to the top. In fact, Jesus said, "Whoever wishes to become great among you shall be your servant." It is by serving that we become great.

The True Test

Jesus once told a story about a very foolish investor, a man who laid up his treasure in the wrong place:

> The land of a certain rich man was very productive. And he began reasoning to himself, "What shall I do, since I have no place to store my crops?" And he said, "This is what I will do: I will tear down my barns and build larger ones, and there I will store all my grain and my goods. And I will say to my soul, 'Soul, you have many goods laid up for many years to come; take your ease, eat, drink and be merry.'" But God said to him, "You fool! This very night your soul is required of you; and now who will own what you have prepared?" So is the man who lays up treasure for himself, and is not rich toward God (Luke 12:16-21).

Obviously, had the wealthy man been "rich toward God," he would not have laid up "treasure for himself," building bigger earthly barns where he could store his abundant crops. Had he been "rich toward God," he would have considered the fact that his bumper crops were a blessing from God. Thus, he had responsibility to steward his blessing.

Did God bless him so that he could retire early and live a life of ease and luxury? Apparently not, since he was destined to die soon. Thus we can only conclude that God blessed him to be a blessing before he died. Had he laid up his treasure in heaven, God would not have considered him to be a fool, but very wise. But he was not "rich toward God." That is, he really had no relationship with God, and it was proven by what he did with what God had entrusted to him.

Our stewardship is indeed a litmus test, if not *the* litmus test, of our relationship with God. Those who are heaven-bound act

> **Those who are heaven-bound act like they are heaven-bound.**

like they are heaven-bound. Those who are *not* acting like they are heaven-bound, but like the rich fool in Jesus' story, are *not* heaven-bound.

Jesus couldn't have made this clearer as He taught His disciples during His Sermon on the Mount, telling them:

> Do not lay up for yourselves treasures upon earth, where moth and rust destroy, and where thieves break in and steal. But lay up for yourselves treasures in heaven, where neither moth nor rust destroys, and where thieves do not break in or steal; for where your treasure is, there will your heart be also. The lamp of the body is the eye; if therefore your eye is clear, your whole body will be full of light. But if your eye is bad, your whole body will be full of darkness. If therefore the light that is in you is darkness, how great is the darkness! No one can serve two masters; for either he will hate the one and love the other, or he will hold to one and despise the other. You cannot serve God and mammon (Matt. 6:19-24).

Jesus was not contrasting committed Christians with uncommitted Christians. Rather, He was contrasting those who do and do not have a relationship with God—as revealed by where they are storing up their treasures.

Note that in Jesus' contrast of two people, one person lays up treasure on earth because his heart is not in heaven. The other lays up treasure in heaven because that is where his heart is. One is full of darkness, that is, ignorance of the truth, while the other is full of light, that is, knowledge of the truth. One has a "bad eye," a common Hebrew idiom for a "greedy heart" (see Prov. 28:22; Matt. 20:15)[1], while the other has a "clear eye," the opposite of the "bad eye," thus signifying a non-greedy heart. One person's god is money, and therefore God is *not* his God, as Jesus said that it is impossible to serve God and money. The other person's master *is* God, as evidenced by the fact that money is not his master.

These two contrasted people are polar opposites.

Clearly, the person who is laying up his treasure on earth—the one whose heart is not in heaven but on earth, who is full of darkness, whose heart is greedy, and whose god is not God but money—is *not* a Christian. And for this reason, anyone who is not laying up treasure in heaven should be gravely concerned about his or her relationship with God.

Keep in mind that it is quite possible, if one has an abundance, to tithe and still lay up lots of earthly treasure. Remember that the Pharisees scrupulously tithed, but they were also lovers of money who were ultimately cast into hell (see Matt. 5:20; 23:15, 23, 33; Luke 16:14; 18:12).

In the final analysis, if we obey Jesus' commandments in regard to our financial stewardship, it is a matter of faith. If we believe in Jesus then we'll do what He says, and we'll reap the benefit of His promises.

The Divine Program

Scripture promises that we will not only be rewarded in the next life for our earthly giving, but also in this life as well. Writing to the Corinthian believers about their promised offering for the suffering saints in Jerusalem, Paul declared:

---

[1] The *King James Version* translates Proverbs 28:22, Matthew 6:23 and Matthew 20:15 to all include the expression "evil eye." Both Greek words translated "evil" in Matthew 6:23 and 20:15 are the same: *poneros.*

Now this I say, he who sows sparingly shall also reap sparingly; and he who sows bountifully shall also reap bountifully (2 Cor. 9:6).

But was he speaking only of reaping in heaven? No, Paul continued:

God is able to make all grace abound to you, that always having all sufficiency in everything, you may have an abundance for every good deed…. Now He who supplies seed to the sower and bread for food, will supply and multiply your seed for sowing and increase the harvest of your righteousness; you will be enriched in everything for all liberality, which through us is producing thanksgiving to God (2 Cor. 9:8, 10-11).

Those who give can expect to receive "an abundance for every good deed," a multiplication of their "seed for sowing," and an enrichment that makes possible more "liberality." Obviously, according to Paul, the blessing of reaping in this life is not so we can disobey God and lay up treasures on earth. Rather it is so we can sow more, and ultimately lay up more treasure in heaven. What a blessing! And this reveals that God is a very good investor himself, as He invests in those who prove to be good investments! He will help us become *forever rich* if we'll just get with the program.

Last Words

In summary, here are the seven principles for becoming *forever rich*:

1.) Your life is a journey to stand before Jesus, the Venture Capitalist before whom you will have to give an account for everything He's loaned to you—your time, talents and treasures. That will be your most important day, so prepare for it every day of your life.

2.) You are among the world's wealthy elite. So learn contentment and remember, "To whom much is given, much is required."

3.) Debt can be good or bad for you. Eliminate all debt that is not likely to increase your earthly and heavenly wealth.

4.) Self-dispossess. Scale down in Disneyland in order to wisely transfer earthly assets to heaven.

5.) Live frugally. Live simply.

6.) Leverage your time, skills and resources intelligently for maximum gain. But don't become a manure-shoveling maniac.

7.) Give intelligently. Give first to truly poor believers, the "least of these," which is the means to laying up treasure in heaven. Remember that the best way to help those who can work is to give them opportunity to work, lifting themselves.

Your treasure is hidden in the field. Buy the field! Be *forever rich!*

Earn all you can, save all you can, give all you can.
— John Wesley

But when the Son of Man comes in His glory, and all the angels with Him, then He will sit on His glorious throne. And all the nations will be gathered before Him; and He will separate them from one another, as the shepherd separates the sheep from the goats; and He will put the sheep on His right, and the goats on the left. Then the King will say to those on His right, "Come, you who are blessed of My Father, inherit the kingdom prepared for you from the foundation of the world. For I was hungry, and you gave Me something to eat; I was thirsty, and you gave Me drink; I was a stranger, and you invited Me in; naked, and you clothed Me; I was sick, and you visited Me; I was in prison, and you came to Me."

Then the righteous will answer Him, saying, "Lord, when did we see You hungry, and feed You, or thirsty, and give You drink? And when did we see You a stranger, and invite You in, or naked, and clothe You? And when did we see You sick, or in prison, and come to You?"

And the King will answer and say to them, "Truly I say to you, to the extent that you did it to one of these brothers of Mine, even the least of them, you did it to Me."

Then He will also say to those on His left, "Depart from Me, accursed ones, into the eternal fire which has been prepared for the devil and his angels; for I was hungry, and you gave Me nothing to eat; I was thirsty, and you gave Me nothing to drink; I was a stranger, and you did not invite Me in; naked, and you did not clothe Me; sick, and in prison, and you did not visit Me."

Then they themselves also will answer, saying, "Lord, when did we see You hungry, or thirsty, or a stranger, or naked, or sick, or in prison, and did not take care of You?"

Then He will answer them, saying, "Truly I say to you, to the extent that you did not do it to one of the least of these, you did not do it to Me." And these will go away into eternal punishment, but the righteous into eternal life (Matt. 25:31-46).

And the multitudes were questioning him [John the Baptist], saying, "Then what shall we do?" And he would answer and say to them, "Let the man who has two tunics share with him who has none; and let him who has food do likewise" (Luke 3:10-11).

Also by David Servant...

Forgive Me for Waiting So Long to Tell You This
Searching for a respectful way to share the gospel with a friend or loved one? Give them a copy of this book. In an easy-to-understand style, David Servant presents a convincing and biblical viewpoint that provokes readers to look at themselves, Jesus Christ, and their eternal destiny. (ISBN 096-296-2503, 132 pages, Paperback, $6.95)

The Disciple-Making Minister
Biblical Principles for Fruitfulness and Multiplication
David Servant has been ministering to Christian leaders in conferences around the world for over two decades. From his experience of speaking to tens of thousands of pastors in over forty countries, he has compiled biblical teaching in this book that addresses the most important issues that Christian leaders are facing today. (ISBN 096-296-2585) 489 pages, Paperback, $19.95)

HeavenWord Daily
HeavenWord Daily guides you through the New Testament following a unique reading plan that will make your daily devotions even more interesting and enriching. *HeavenWord Daily* is not a fluff devotional, but rather a "motivational devotional," full of insight and inspiration. (ISBN 978-0-9827656-0-9) 535 pages, Hardcover, $15.00)

Through the Needle's Eye
An Impossible Journey Made Possible by God
In this book, David Servant considers everything that Jesus, as well as every author of the Old and New Testaments, taught in regard to stewardship. His conclusions are not easy to disregard. Although impossible by pure human effort, the journey through the needle's eye is possible with God! (ISBN 096-296-2592) 269 pages, Paperback, $17.95)

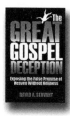

The Great Gospel Deception
Exposing the False Promise of Heaven Without Holiness
In this eye-opening book, David Servant takes a close look at what the New Testament actually teaches about saving faith, God's transforming grace, and "the holiness without which no one will see the Lord" (Hebrews 12:14). (ISBN 096-296-2578) 240 pages, Paperback, $17.95)

Need a Daily 7-Minute Spiritual Boost?

HeavenWord TV is just for you!

Sign up today at HeavenWord.TV to start receiving David Servant's daily video devotional, HeavenWord 7. Every week-day morning, you'll find an email in your inbox with a link to that day's 7-minute video teaching. You can be fed spiritually while you enjoy your breakfast, Monday through Friday, as David teaches verse-by-verse through the entire New Testament chronologically.

You can also subscribe to the identical teaching in a weekly half-hour format, called HeavenWord TV, that is perfect for Bible studies, Sunday School classes and house churches. Or, view any 7-minute or half-hour episode of your choosing in the archives at HeavenWord.TV, or subscribe via iTunes.

Don't delay, sign up today! Your first video link will be waiting for you when you awake on the next weekday!

www.HeavenWord.TV

Heaven's Family
Your Love-Link to the "Least of These"

Heaven's Family serves as a love-link to the "least of these," those of whom Jesus spoke in His foretelling of the judgment of the sheep and the goats in Matthew 25.

Through our many focused funds, we assist poor Christians who are facing even more daunting challenges than poverty, such as persecution, hunger, unsafe water, natural disasters, widowhood, illness, orphanhood, physical handicaps, and more. We also establish micro-banks that help enterprising believers lift themselves from poverty through small-business loans.

Through our orphan care initiative, *Orphan's Tear*, we serve nearly 1,000 orphans living in more than 50 Christian orphanages in 8 nations.

In every case, 100% of what is contributed to a focused fund or *Orphan's Tear* is sent overseas to meet the pressings needs for which it was given. All administrative costs are paid through gifts to our general fund.

Through the teaching arm of our ministry, *Shepherd Serve*, we're equipping tens of thousands of Christian leaders by means of teaching found on our website (in a growing number of languages), and also through the distribution of a 500-page equipping manual titled, *The Disciple-Making Minister*, now distributed in more than 20 languages.

Please visit us at HeavensFamily.org to learn more. We're here to serve as your love-link to the "least of these."